Essential American Idioms

Second Edition

MAKES IDIOMS, CLICHÉS,
AND PHRASES EASY TO
UNDERSTAND AND TO USE

RICHARD A. SPEARS, PH.D.

NTC Publishing Group

Library of Congress Cataloging-in-Publication Data

Spears, Richard A.
    Essential American idioms / Richard A. Spears. — 2nd ed.
       p.   cm. — (NTC reference)
    ISBN 0-8442-0467-6
      1. English language—United States—Idioms—Dictionaries.
    2. Americanisms—Dictionaries.   I. Title.   II. Series.
    PE2839.S63   1999
    423'.1—dc21   98-56009
                                          CIP

Cover design by Nick Panos
Interior design by Terry Stone

Published by NTC Publishing Group
A division of NTC/Contemporary Publishing Group, Inc.
4255 West Touhy Avenue, Lincolnwood (Chicago), Illinois 60646-1975 U.S.A.
Copyright © 1999 by NTC/Contemporary Publishing Group, Inc.
Manufactured in the United States of America
International Standard Book Number: 0-8442-0467-6

   00 01 02 03 04 LB 18 17 16 15 14 13 12 11 10 9 8 7 6 5 4 3 2

Contents

About This Dictionary

Every language has phrases that cannot be understood literally. Even if you know the meanings of all the words in such a phrase and you understand the grammar completely, the total meaning of the phrase may still be confusing. English has many thousands of such idiomatic expressions. This dictionary is a selection of frequently encountered idiomatic expressions found in everyday American English. The collection is small enough to serve as a useful study guide for learners, and large enough to serve as a reference for daily use.

The second edition is an entirely new compilation and contains 1,700 idiomatic phrases. This edition also has a Phrase-Finder Index that allows the user to find a particular idiom by looking up any major word in the phrase.

This dictionary should prove useful for people who are learning how to understand idiomatic English, for the hearing impaired, and for all speakers of English who want to know more about the language.

Guide to the Use of the Dictionary

Expressions are listed in an absolute alphabetical order that ignores hyphens, spaces, and other punctuation. Each idiomatic phrase is given in its normal form and word order, but the alphabetizing scheme ignores the articles *a*, *an*, and *the* when these words come at the beginning of an entry. Each entry or sense has at least two examples, printed in *italics*.

Terms and Symbols

☐ (a box) marks the beginning of an example.

⊤ (a box containing a T) marks the beginning of an example having a different word order from the order shown in the entry head.

ALSO: introduces an additional variant form within an entry, which is related to the main entry but has a slightly different meaning or form.

see means to turn to the entry indicated.

see also means to consult the entry indicated for additional information or to find expressions similar in form or meaning to the entry head where the "see also" instruction appeared.

see under means to turn to the entry indicated and look for the phrase you are seeking within that entry.

above par better than average or normal. □ *His work is above par, so he should get paid better.* □ *Your chances of winning the game are a little above par.*

above reproach not deserving of blame or criticism. □ *Some politicians behave as though they are above reproach.* □ *You must accept your punishment. You are not above reproach.*

Act your age! Behave more maturely! (A rebuke for someone who is acting childish. Often said to a child who is acting like an even younger child.) □ *Johnny was squirming around and pinching his sister. His mother finally said, "Johnny, act your age!"* □ *CHILD: Aw, come on! Let me see your book! MARY: Be quiet and act your age. Don't be such a baby.*

add insult to injury to make a bad situation worse; to hurt the feelings of a person who has already been hurt. (A cliché.) □ *First, the basement flooded, and then, to add insult to injury, a pipe burst in the kitchen.* □ *My car barely started this morning, and, to add insult to injury, I got a flat tire in the driveway.*

advanced in years old. □ *Mrs. Sanders is considerably advanced in years, but she is well able to take care of herself.* □ *The librarian was a kind gentleman, quite advanced in years.*

affinity for someone or something a strong preference for something; a strong liking for something. □ *Cats have an affinity for seafood.* □ *Mary's affinity for classical music accounts for her large collection of recordings.*

again and again repeatedly; again and even more. □ *I like going to the beach, and I go back again and again.* □ *He knocked on the door again and again until I finally answered.*

against the clock in a race with time; in a great hurry to get something done before a particular time. □ *Don't bother me. I'm*

1

working against the clock to finish this project by noon. □ *In a race against the clock, they rushed the special medicine to the hospital.*

against the grain against someone's natural direction or inclination. (Refers to the lay of the grain of wood. Against the grain is perpendicular to the lay of the grain.) □ *Don't expect me to help you cheat. That goes against the grain.* □ *Would it go against the grain for you to call in sick for me?*

ahead of one's time having ideas or attitudes that are too advanced to be acceptable to the society in which one is living. □ *People buy that artist's work now, but his paintings were laughed at when he was alive. He was ahead of his time.* □ *Mary's grandmother was ahead of her time in wanting to study medicine.*

air someone's dirty linen in public to discuss private or embarrassing matters in public, especially when quarreling. □ *John's mother had asked him repeatedly not to air the family's dirty linen in public.* □ *Mr. and Mrs. Johnson are arguing again. Why must they always air their dirty linen in public?*

all in a day's work part of what is expected; typical or normal. □ *I don't particularly like to cook, but it's all in a day's work.* □ *Putting up with rude customers isn't pleasant, but it's all in a day's work.* □ *Cleaning up after other people is all in a day's work for a chambermaid.*

all in all AND **all things considered; on balance** a transition indicating a summary, a generalization, or the announcement of a conclusion. □ *BILL: All in all, this was a fine evening. ALICE: I think so, too.* □ *"Our time at the conference was well spent, all in all," thought Fred.* □ *BILL: How did it go? ALICE: On balance, it went quite well.* □ *BOB: Did the play turn a profit? FRED: I suppose that we made a nice profit, all things considered.*

(all) joking aside When I say the following, I am not kidding or joking any longer. □ *All joking aside, I think you will enjoy your trip to Cleveland.* □ *Joking aside, teenagers can be nice people sometimes.*

(all) over again yet another time; completely repeated again. □ *Do we have to go through the same explanation all over again?* □ *You have to do your assignment over again. You got it wrong the first time.*

all over but the shouting essentially decided and concluded. (An elaboration of *all over,* which means "finished.") □ *The last goal was made just before the final whistle sounded. Tom said, "Well, it's all over but the shouting."* □ *By the time two-thirds of the votes had been counted, it was clear who would win the election. "It's all over but the shouting," said the reporter.*

All right. 1. an indication of agreement or acquiescence. (Often pronounced *aright* in familiar conversation.) □ *FATHER: Do it now, before you forget. BILL: All right.* □ *TOM: Please remember to bring me back a pizza. SALLY: All right, but I get to eat some of it.* **2.** a shout of agreement or encouragement. (Usually **All right!**) □ *ALICE: Come on, let's give Sally some encouragement. FRED: All right, Sally! Keep it up! You can do it!* □ *"That's the way to go! All right!" shouted various members of the audience.*

All systems are go. an indication that everything is ready or that things are going along as planned. (Borrowed from the jargon used during America's early space exploration.) □ *BILL: Can we leave now? Is the car gassed up and ready? TOM: All systems are go. Let's get going.* □ *SALLY: Are you all rested up for the track meet? MARY: Yes. All systems are go.*

all there alert, aware, and mentally sound. (Usually in the phrase *not all there,* meaning "not mentally sound.") □ *After talking with Larry today, I get the feeling that he's not quite all there.* □ *You do such foolish things sometimes! I wonder if you're all there.*

all things considered See all in all.

all walks of life all social, economic, and ethnic groups. □ *We saw people there from all walks of life.* □ *The people who came to the art exhibit represented all walks of life.*

the **almighty dollar** the U.S. dollar, worshiped as a god; money, viewed as more important and powerful than anything else. □ *Bill was a slave to the almighty dollar.* □ *It's the almighty dollar that drives the whole country.*

Am I glad to see you! I am very glad to see you! (Not a question. There is a stress on *I* and another on *you.*) □ *BOB: Well, I finally got here! JOHN: Bob! Am I glad to see you! We were afraid that you were lost.* □ *TOM (as Bill opens the door): Here I am, Bill. What's wrong? BILL: Boy, am I glad to see you! Come on in. The hot water heater exploded, and I need your help.*

and so forth and similar things or actions; and continuing on in the same way; and so on. □ *She told me everything about her kids, and so on and so forth.* □ *I heard about problems at work and so forth.*

and so on and similar things or actions; and continuing on in the same way. □ *He told me about all his health problems, including his arthritis and so on.* □ *I need some help getting ready for dinner, setting the table, and so on.*

and the like and similar things or people. □ *I eat hamburgers, hot dogs, and the like.* □ *I bought shirts, pants, socks, and the like.*

answer the call to die. (A euphemism.) □ *Grandma answered the call and went to heaven.* □ *Our dear brother has answered the call and gone to his eternal rest.*

answer the door [after hearing the doorbell or a knock] to go or come to the door to see who is there. □ *Would you please answer the door? I am busy.* □ *I wish someone would answer the door. I can't wait all day.*

Anything you say. Yes.; I agree.; I will do as you wish. □ *MARY: Will you please take this over to the cleaners? BILL: Sure, anything you say.* □ *SALLY: You're going to finish this before you leave tonight, aren't you? MARY: Anything you say.*

the **apple of someone's eye** someone's favorite person or thing; a boyfriend or a girlfriend; a person or a thing that someone wants. (A person or a thing that has caught someone's eye or attracted someone's attention.) □ *Tom is the apple of Mary's eye. She thinks he's great.* □ *John's new stereo is the apple of his eye.*

as a duck takes to water easily and naturally. (Refers to baby ducks, who seem to be able to swim the first time they enter the water.) □ *She took to singing, just as a duck takes to water.* □ *Our baby adapted to bottle-feeding as a duck takes to water.*

as a matter of fact truly; in fact; factually speaking; referring to the facts. □ *As a matter of fact, I am old enough to know what it was like in 1929.* □ *I was in Cleveland myself last week, as a matter of fact.*

as a rule in general; usually. □ *As a rule, men should wear tuxedos at formal parties.* □ *As a rule, the bus picks me up at 7:30, but occasionally it is late.*

as _____ as they come having as much of a quality as it is possible to have. □ *John is as dumb as they come. He just doesn't think.* □ *Mary is as clever as they come.*

(as) far as I know AND **to the best of my knowledge** an expression of basic, but not well informed, agreement, together with an indication that the speaker's knowledge may not be adequate. □ *TOM: Is this brand of computer any good? CLERK: This is the very best one there is, as far as I know.* □ *FRED: Are the trains on time? TICKET AGENT: To the best of my knowledge, all the trains are on time today.* □ *BILL: Are we just about there? TOM: Far as I know. BILL: I thought you'd been there before. TOM: Never.*

(as) far as I'm concerned 1. from my point of view; as concerns my interests. □ *BOB: Isn't this cake good? ALICE: Yes, indeed. As far as I'm concerned, this is the best cake I have ever eaten.* □ *TOM: I think I'd better go. BOB: As far as I'm concerned, you all can leave now.* **2.** Okay, as it concerns my interests. □ *ALICE: Can I send this package on to your sister? JOHN: As far as I'm concerned.* □ *JANE: Do you mind if I put this coat in the closet? JOHN: Far as I'm concerned. It's not mine.*

as for in regard to; concerning; relative to. □ *"As for you," the teacher yelled at the rude pupil, "you can go to the principal's office."* □ *As for the window you broke, you'll have to pay for it out of your allowance.*

as I see it AND **in my opinion; in my view** the way I think about it. □ *TOM: This matter is not as bad as some would make it out to be. ALICE: Yes. This whole affair has been overblown, as I see it.* □ *BOB: You're as wrong as can be. JOHN: In my view, you are wrong.*

ask for the moon to ask for too much; to make great demands; to ask for something that is difficult or impossible to obtain. (Not literal.) □ *When you're trying to get a job, it's unwise to ask for the moon.* □ *Please lend me the money. I'm not asking for the moon!*

as long as 1. AND **so long as** provided that . . . ; on the condition that . . . □ *I will pay you extra money so long as you promise to finish the job tomorrow.* □ *As long as you do what you are told, everything will be fine.* **2.** AND **so long as** since; given the fact that . . . □ *As long as you are going to the kitchen, please bring me* *some popcorn.* □ *As long as I have to take this check to the bank, I can also take the laundry to the Laundromat.* **3.** during or throughout the period of time that . . . □ *As long as I have worked here, we have always had half-hour lunch breaks.* □ *As long as we have lived here, the basement has never flooded.*

as such [being] the way something is; as someone or something is. □ *I cannot accept your manuscript as such. It needs revisions.* □ *You are new here, and as such, I will have to train you.*

assume liability to accept the responsibility for paying a cost. □ *Mr. Smith assumed liability for his son's student loans.* □ *The store assumed liability for the injured customer's hospital bill.*

as the saying goes as it is often said; quoting a saying, maxim, or wise remark. □ *As the saying goes, it was worth doing once.* □ *All's well that ends well, as the saying goes.*

as usual as is the normal or typical situation. □ *John ordered eggs for breakfast as usual.* □ *He stood quietly as usual, waiting for the bus to come.*

as well 1. also; in addition. □ *Could I have some more potatoes as well?* □ *I'm feeling tired, and dizzy as well.* **2.** equally well; in as good or as satisfactory a way. □ *The boss is very kind to his friends. I wish he would treat his employees as well!* □ *Mary is the best singer in the class. No one else in the class sings as well.*

as well as 1. in addition to someone or something. □ *The older children, as well as the younger ones, enjoy going to the zoo.* □ *I'm studying biology and chemistry, as well as history.* **2.** in as good or as satisfactory a way as someone or something; in as good or as satisfactory a way as someone or something does something. □ *Mary's parents treated me as well as they treated her.* □ *I did as well as you on the test.* □ *I did as well as you did on the test.*

as we speak just now; at this very moment. (This has almost reached cliché status.) □ *"I'm sorry, sir, but you're too late," said the agent at the gate. "The plane is taking off as we speak."* □ *TOM: Waiter, where is my steak? It's taking a long time. WAITER: It is being grilled as we speak, sir—just as you requested.*

at any rate in any case; anyway. □ *At any rate, what were we talking about?* □ *At any rate, I don't think you should quit your job.*

at a premium at a high price; priced high because of something special. □ *Sally bought the shoes at a premium because they were of very high quality.* □ *This model of car is selling at a premium because so many people want to buy it.*

at bay at a distance. □ *I have to keep the bill collectors at bay until I get my check.* □ *The wolves will not remain at bay for very long.*

at death's door near death. □ *I was so ill that I was at death's door.* □ *The family dog was at death's door for three days, and then it finally died.*

at ease without worry or anxiety. □ *The performer is at ease on the stage.* □ *After she had met a few people, Mary felt at ease with the group.*

(at) full blast as fast or as strong as possible; with as much volume or pressure as possible. □ *Stop playing your stereo at full blast.* □ *The furnace is working full blast, and it's still cold in here!*

at full tilt at full speed; as fast as possible. □ *The driver sped down the road at full tilt.* □ *The runner raced at full tilt toward the finish line.*

at half-mast [of a flag] hung below the top of a flagpole, nearer the midpoint of the pole. □ *The company flag flew at half-mast in honor of the owner's death.* □ *The flag was flown at half-mast for a week following the president's death.*

at hazard risked; in danger; at risk. □ *He is not willing to have much of his money at hazard in the stock market.* □ *Your entire life is at hazard unless you wear a helmet when you ride your bicycle.*

at its best See at one's best.

at last finally; after a long wait. □ *The train has come at last.* □ *At last, we have found something to eat.*

at liberty without a job; free from the responsibilities of working. (A euphemism.) □ *INTERVIEWER: What position do you currently hold? JOB CANDIDATE: I am currently at liberty.* □ *You may consider yourself at liberty. We can no longer continue to employ you.*

at liberty to do something free to do something; permitted to do something. □ *The general was not at liberty to divulge the military's plans.* □ *You are at liberty to leave anytime you wish.*

at loggerheads in opposition; at an impasse; in a quarrel. □ *Mr. and Mrs. Franklin have been at loggerheads for years.* □ *The two political parties were at loggerheads throughout the legislative session.*

at one's best AND **at its best** of the utmost quality; representing one's or its highest level of quality or achievement. □ *This restaurant serves gourmet food at its best.* □ *The singer was at her best when she performed ballads.*

at one's wit's end at the limits of one's mental resources. □ *I'm at my wit's end with this problem. I cannot figure it out.* □ *Tom could do no more. He was at his wit's end.*

at peace 1. peaceful; resting; calm; tranquil. □ *Finally the storm ended, and the valley was at peace once more.* □ *I will not be at peace until I find out what really happened.* **2.** dead, and therefore no longer suffering. (A euphemism.) □ *After struggling with cancer for many long months, Steven is finally at peace.* □ *Our dear, departed brother is now at peace.*

at play [at this moment] involved in playing. □ *The children are at play, and I am doing household chores.* □ *Whether I am at work or at play, I try to be pleasant to people.*

at random by chance; haphazardly. □ *The lottery numbers are chosen at random.* □ *As a prank, the children dialed phone numbers at random.*

at regular intervals at points that are equal in distance apart. □ *You will find service stations at regular intervals along the highway.* □ *There are street lights at regular intervals on the main street of the town.*

at rest 1. not moving; not active. □ *After the hectic day, the office was finally at rest at 8:00 P.M.* □ *Do not remove your seat belt until the plane is at rest at the terminal gate.* **2.** dead. (A euphemism.) □ *After a long, weary life, Emily is at rest.* □ *There he is, at rest in his coffin.*

at risk in a situation where there is risk or hazard; in danger. □ *I refuse to put my family's welfare at risk by quitting my job.* □ *Your whole future is at risk if you don't stop smoking.*

at sea on the sea; away on a voyage on the ocean. □ *The ship is at sea now, and you can't disembark.* □ *I spent many happy days at sea on my cruise.*

at sea (about something) confused; lost and bewildered. □ *Mary is all at sea about getting married.* □ *When it comes to higher math, John is totally at sea.*

at sea level located at the same level as the surface of the sea. □ *It is easier to breathe at sea level than in the mountains.* □ *Boats on the ocean are at sea level, but those on rivers are not.*

attached to someone or something fond of someone or something. □ *John is really attached to his old-fashioned ideas.* □ *I'm really attached to this old house.*

at the bottom of the ladder at the lowest level of pay and status. □ *Most people start work at the bottom of the ladder.* □ *When Anne got fired, she had to start all over again at the bottom of the ladder.*

at the end of one's rope at the limits of one's endurance. □ *I'm at the end of my rope! I just can't go on this way!* □ *These kids are driving me out of my mind. I'm at the end of my rope.*

at the forefront (of something) AND **in the forefront (of something)** in the most important place; at the place of greatest activity. □ *I interviewed Max Brown, the director who is in the forefront of the movie industry.* □ *The university I go to is at the forefront of computer technology.*

at the height of something at the most intense or forceful point or stage in something. □ *At the height of his career, Tom was known around the world.* □ *At the height of the party, there were 50 people present.*

at the helm (of something) in the position of being in control of something. □ *The president is at the helm of the company.* □ *Things will go well with Anne at the helm.*

at the last minute at the last possible chance. □ *Please don't make reservations at the last minute.* □ *Why do you ask all your questions at the last minute?*

at (the) most no more than [some amount]; as the highest possible count or estimate. □ *"How far away is the beach?" "Ten miles* *at most."* □ *At the most, there were only fifteen people in the audience.*

at the outset at the very beginning. □ *At the outset, we were told everything we had to do.* □ *I learned at the outset of the project that I was to lead it.*

at the outside at the very most; absolutely no more than [some amount]. □ *The car repairs will cost $300 at the outside.* □ *I'll be there in three weeks at the outside.*

at the present time now. (Almost a cliché.) □ *"We are very sorry to report that we are unable to fill your order at the present time,"* stated the little note on the order form. □ *MARY: How long will it be until we can be seated? WAITER: There are no tables available at the present time, madam. MARY: But, how long?*

at the rear of something located at the back part of something. □ *I keep my tools at the rear of my garage.* □ *There's a creek at the rear of my property.*

at the top of one's lungs See at the top of one's voice.

at the top of one's voice AND **at the top of one's lungs** with a very loud voice; as loudly as one can possibly speak or yell. □ *Bill called to Mary at the top of his voice.* □ *How can I work when you're all talking at the top of your lungs?*

at the zenith of something at the highest point of something; at the pinnacle of something. □ *At the zenith of his career, the teacher died suddenly.* □ *The scientist was at the zenith of her career when she made her discovery.*

avail oneself of something to help oneself by making use of something that is available. □ *We availed ourselves of Tom's goodwill and let him repair the fence.* □ *The campers eagerly availed themselves of their first chance in a week to take a shower.*

avenue of escape the pathway or route along which someone or something escapes. □ *The open window was the bird's only avenue of escape from the house.* □ *Bill saw that his one avenue of escape was through the back door.*

a **babe in the woods** a naive or innocent person; an inexperienced person. □ *Bill is a babe in the woods when it comes to dealing with plumbers.* □ *As a painter, Mary is fine, but she's a babe in the woods as a musician.*

back to square one back to the beginning; back to the starting point or place. □ *This solution didn't work, so it's back to square one.* □ *We have to start all over again. Back to square one.*

bag and baggage with one's luggage; with all one's possessions. □ *Sally showed up at our door bag and baggage one Sunday morning.* □ *All right, if you won't pay the rent, out with you, bag and baggage!*

The **ball is in your court.** It is now your turn to do something.; You are expected to act or do something at this point. □ *They have sent the signed contract back. The ball is in your court.* □ *The ball is in your court. Tom has done everything you asked him to do.*

balls of one's feet the bottom part of the feet just under the toes. □ *Mary got blisters around the balls of her feet from playing tennis.* □ *The dancer balanced on the balls of his feet.*

ball someone or something up to mess someone or something up. □ *I hope I don't ball it up again!* ⊤ *You ball up another contract, and you are finished!*

the **bare something** the smallest amount of something possible; only the most basic and essential portion of something. □ *Bob did the bare minimum of work to pass the class.* □ *Food, clothing, and shelter are the bare necessities of life.*

barking up the wrong tree making the wrong choice; asking the wrong person; following the wrong course. (Refers to a hunting dog that has chased a creature up a tree, but stands barking or howling at the wrong tree.) □ *If you think I'm the guilty person, you're barking up the wrong tree.* □ *The baseball players blamed their bad record on the pitcher, but they were barking up the wrong tree.*

be a big frog in a small pond to be an important person in the midst of people who are not very important; to be an important person within a small or limited group or area. □ *The trouble with Tom is that he's a big frog in a small pond. He needs more competition.* □ *I'd rather be a big frog in a small pond than the opposite.*

be a gas to be wild or funny. □ *You should have been at Susan's party last night. It was a gas.* □ *That movie was such a gas. I haven't laughed so hard in ages.*

bear in mind that . . . to remember something; to consider something. □ *Bear in mind that the trip will be expensive.* □ *I asked the music teacher to bear in mind that I am just a beginner.*

be a slave to something to be under the control of something; to be controlled by something. □ *Mary is a slave to her job.* □ *Bill is a slave to his drug addiction.*

beat a path to someone's door [for people] to come to someone in great numbers. (As if so many people come to see a person that they wear down a pathway leading up to the person's door.) □ *I have a product so good that everyone is beating a path to my door.* □ *If you really become famous, people will beat a path to your door.*

beating a dead horse continuing to fight a battle that has been won; continuing to argue a point that is settled. (A dead horse will not run no matter how hard it is beaten.) □ *Stop arguing! You have won your point. You are just beating a dead horse.* □ *Oh, be quiet. Stop beating a dead horse.*

Beat it! Go away!; Get out! (Slang.) □ *BILL: Sorry I broke your radio. BOB: Get out of here! Beat it!* □ *"Beat it, you kids! Go play somewhere else!" yelled the storekeeper.*

Beats me. See It beats me.

beat the gun to manage to do something before the ending signal. (Originally from sports, referring to making a goal in the last seconds of a game.) □ *The ball beat the gun and dropped* *through the hoop just in time.* □ *Tom tried to beat the gun, but he was one second too slow.*

be conspicuous by one's absence to have one's absence (from an event) noticed. □ *We missed you last night. You were conspicuous by your absence.* □ *How could the bride's father miss the reception? He was certainly conspicuous by his absence.*

be death on something to be very harmful to something. □ *The salt they put on the roads in the winter is death on cars.* □ *That teacher is death on slow learners.*

be descended from someone or some creature to come from an ancestor. □ *Anne is descended from a family of British shopkeepers.* □ *Mary is descended from Irish peasants.*

be down with something See come down with something.

been had been duped; been cheated. (Slang.) □ *I may have been had, but I'll get even.* □ *Tom knew he had been had when the cheap watch stopped running the day after he bought it.*

Been keeping cool. See I've been keeping cool.

be game to be ready for action; to be agreeable to participating in something. □ *"I'm game," David replied, when I suggested we go bowling.* □ *We're going to the park to play football. Are you game?*

behind schedule having failed to do something by the time listed on a schedule. □ *We have to hurry and finish soon because we are behind schedule.* □ *The project is behind schedule. Very late, in fact.*

Behind you! Look behind you!; There is danger behind you! □ *"Behind you!" shouted Tom, just as a car raced past and nearly knocked Mary over.* □ *Alice shouted, "Behind you!" just as the pickpocket made off with Fred's wallet.*

believe it or not [you may] choose to believe this or not to believe it. (Said when mentioning something that may sound surprising.) □ *Believe it or not, I just got home from work.* □ *I'm over fifty years old, believe it or not.*

Believe you me! You can believe what I am telling you!; I am being absolutely truthful! □ *It's going to be hot today, believe you me!* □ *Believe you me, taxes are going to bankrupt us all.*

below average lower or worse than average. □ *Tom's strength is below average for a child his size.* □ *Dad asked why my grades are below average.*

below par not as good as average or normal. □ *I feel a little below par today. I think I am getting a cold.* □ *His work is below par, and he is paid too much money.*

Be my guest. Please do what you wish to do.; Please proceed ahead of me.; After you. (A polite way of indicating that one should go first, help oneself, or take the last one of something.) □ *MARY: I would just love to have some more cake, but there is only one piece left. SALLY: Be my guest. MARY: Wow! Thanks!* □ *JANE: Here's Mr. Smith's office. Who should go in first? BILL: Be my guest. I'll wait out here. JANE: Why don't you go first?*

bend someone's ear to talk to someone, perhaps annoyingly. (Not literal. The person's ear is not touched.) □ *Tom is over there, bending Jane's ear about something.* □ *I'm sorry. I didn't mean to bend your ear for an hour.*

bend the rules 1. to allow a rule to be violated in a very minor way, often for a good reason. □ *You are supposed to pay today, but I can bend the rules a little and allow you to pay tomorrow.* □ *No children are allowed in here, but we'll bend the rules so your daughter can visit you.* **2.** to cheat. (A euphemism.) □ *Even as a child, he would bend the rules in order to win.* □ *It became apparent that the senator had bent the rules when filing her taxes.*

the **benefit of the doubt** a judgment in one's favor when the evidence is neither for one nor against one. □ *I was right between a B and an A. I got the benefit of the doubt—an A.* □ *I thought I should have had the benefit of the doubt, but the judge made me pay a fine.*

bent on doing something resolved to do something; intent on doing something. □ *The kids were bent on going to the amusement park, rain or shine.* □ *The boss is bent on increasing production this quarter.*

be of the persuasion that . . . to hold a belief that something is true. □ *Anne is of the persuasion that education is more important than wealth.* □ *The paranoid man was of the persuasion that aliens lived among us.*

be old hat to be old-fashioned; to be outmoded. (Refers to anything—except a hat—that is out of style, just as an old hat would be.) □ *That's a silly idea. It's old hat.* □ *Nobody does that anymore. That's just old hat.*

be on the safe side to be safe; to be cautious; [to do something just] in case it is necessary; to be very well prepared. □ *To be on the safe side, carry some extra money in your shoe.* □ *I like to be on the safe side and stay in my hotel room at night.*

beside oneself very upset; distressed. □ *She was beside herself over breaking the antique vase.* □ *The whole family was beside itself with grief.*

be swimming in something to be engulfed by an excess of something, as if it were a flood. □ *The war-torn city was swimming in blood.* □ *I am just swimming in paperwork.*

be thankful for small blessings to be grateful for any small benefits or advantages one has, especially in a generally difficult situation. □ *We have very little money, but we must be thankful for small blessings. At least we have enough food.* □ *Bob was badly injured in the accident, but at least he's still alive. Let's be thankful for small blessings.*

be that as it may even though that may be true; regardless of that. □ *Your news is interesting, but, be that as it may, we will continue with our planned activities.* □ *Yes, it's cold. Be that as it may, you still must get out of bed and go to school.*

be the black sheep of the family to be the least satisfactory or worst member of a family or group; to be not up to the standard of the rest of the family. (A black sheep is an unwanted offspring in a herd of otherwise white sheep.) □ *Mary is the black sheep of the family. She's always in trouble with the police.* □ *He keeps making a nuisance of himself. What do you expect from the black sheep of the family?*

be the case to be true; to describe an actual situation. □ *I think Bill is a vegetarian, and if that is the case, we should not serve him meat.* □ *Susie believes trees can talk, but that is not the case.*

be the spit and image of someone AND **be the spitting image of someone** to look very much like someone; to resemble someone very closely. □ *John is the spit and image of his father.* □ *I'm not the spitting image of anyone.*

15

be the spitting image of someone See be the spit and image of someone.

be to do something to be obliged to do something; to be expected or directed to do something. □ *Am I to clean up the entire kitchen by myself?* □ *John is to take the money to the bank.*

Better get on my horse. See I'd better get on my horse.

Better keep quiet about it. See Better keep still about it.

Better keep still about it. AND **Better keep quiet about it.** an admonition that a person ought not to tell about or discuss something. □ *MARY: I saw you with Bill last night. JANE: You'd better keep quiet about it.* □ *JANE: Tom found out what you're giving Sally for her birthday. BILL: He had better keep quiet about it!*

better left unsaid [refers to a topic that] should not be discussed; [refers to a thought that] everyone is thinking, but would cause difficulty if talked about in public. (A typical beginning for this phrase might be *It is, That is, The details are,* or even *Some things are.* See the examples.) □ *MARY: I really don't know how to tell you this. BOB: Then don't. Maybe it's better left unsaid.* □ *BILL: I had such a terrible fight with Sally last night. It was just awful. BOB: I don't need to hear all about it. Some things are better left unsaid.*

between a rock and a hard place AND **between the devil and the deep blue sea** in a very difficult position; facing a hard decision. □ *I couldn't make up my mind. I was caught between a rock and a hard place.* □ *He had a dilemma on his hands. He was clearly between the devil and the deep blue sea.*

between jobs unemployed. (A euphemism.) □ *INTERVIEWER: Tell me about your current position. JOB CANDIDATE: I'm between jobs right now.* □ *While Jill was between jobs, she took a computer class at the community college.*

between the devil and the deep blue sea See between a rock and a hard place.

be used to someone or something to be accustomed to someone or something; to be familiar and comfortable with someone or something. (*Something* can be an action of *doing something.*) □ *Bill has lived in Alaska for so long that he is used to the cold.*

□ *Mary is used to the doctor she has, and she doesn't want to change.* □ *I'm not used to waking up so early in the morning!*

beyond one's depth 1. [of someone] in water that is too deep; [of water] too deep for someone. (Literal.) □ *Sally swam out until she was beyond her depth.* □ *Jane swam out into the deep water to get her little brother, even though it was beyond her depth.* **2.** [of someone] involved in something that is too difficult or advanced; [of something] beyond one's understanding or capabilities. □ *I'm beyond my depth in algebra class.* □ *Poor John was involved in a problem that was really beyond his depth.*

beyond one's means more than one can afford. □ *I'm sorry, but this house is beyond our means. Please show us a less expensive one.* □ *Mr. and Mrs. Brown are living beyond their means.*

beyond the shadow of a doubt See without a shadow of a doubt.

Big deal! So what!; It's not important!; Why are you making so much commotion about it? □ *So, I'm late a few minutes! Big deal!* □ *Big deal! Billy spilled his milk. There's more milk!*

the **birds and the bees** human reproduction. (A euphemistic way of referring to human sex and reproduction.) □ *My father taught me about the birds and the bees.* □ *He's twenty years old and doesn't understand about the birds and the bees!*

bite the hand that feeds one to do harm to someone who does good things for one. (Not literal. Refers to the act of a thankless dog.) □ *I'm your mother! How can you bite the hand that feeds you?* □ *She can hardly expect much when she bites the hand that feeds her.*

black and blue bruised; [of skin] showing signs of physical injury. □ *My knee is black and blue because I bumped into the side of my desk yesterday and hurt it.* □ *She was black and blue all over after falling out of the tree.*

the **blind leading the blind** a situation where people who don't know how to do something try to explain it to other people. □ *Tom doesn't know anything about cars, but he's trying to teach Sally how to change the oil. It's a case of the blind leading the blind.* □ *When I tried to show Mary how to use a computer, it was the blind leading the blind.*

blow a fuse 1. to burn out an electrical fuse. □ *The microwave oven blew a fuse, so we had no power.* □ *You'll blow a fuse if you use too many appliances at once.* **2.** to become very angry; to lose one's temper. (Informal.) □ *Bill will blow a fuse when he hears about this.* □ *The boss blew a fuse when the workers all arrived an hour late.*

blow one's nose to drive mucus and other material from one's nose by breathing out through one's nose strongly. □ *Excuse me, I have to blow my nose.* □ *Bill blew his nose into his handkerchief.*

blow someone's cover to reveal someone's true identity or purpose. (Informal or slang.) □ *The spy was very careful not to blow her cover.* □ *I tried to disguise myself, but my dog recognized me and blew my cover.*

bone of contention the subject or point of an argument; an unsettled point of disagreement. (Like a bone that dogs fight over.) □ *We've fought for so long that we've forgotten what the bone of contention is.* □ *The question of building a fence between the houses has become quite a bone of contention.*

born in a barn raised in such a way that one leave doors open and generally behaves in a somewhat disorderly manner. □ *Close the door! Were you born in a barn?* □ *Fred is sloppy and noisy. I think he was born in a barn.*

born out of wedlock born from parents who were not legally married. □ *The young infant had been born out of wedlock.* □ *A large proportion of births each year are of babies born out of wedlock.*

bound for somewhere headed for a specific goal or destination. □ *Bill accidentally got on a bus bound for Miami.* □ *Our baseball team is bound for glory.*

bound hand and foot with hands and feet tied up. □ *The robbers left us bound hand and foot.* □ *We remained bound hand and foot until the maid found us and untied us.*

bound to do something certain to do something. □ *The Mets are bound to win the pennant eventually.* □ *You're bound to publish a novel some day.*

bowl someone over to overwhelm or surprise someone, especially with something good. □ *We were bowled over by the expensive* *wedding gift.* □ *David bowled his parents over with his excellent report card.*

break a code to figure out a code; to decipher a code. □ *The intelligence agents finally broke the enemy's code.* □ *When they broke the code, they were able to decipher messages.*

break a habit AND **break the habit; break one's habit** to end a habit. □ *I was not able to break the habit of snoring.* □ *It's hard to break a habit that you have had for a long time.*

break a law AND **break the law** to fail to obey a law; to act contrary to a law. □ *Lisa broke the law when she drove the wrong way on a one-way street.* □ *If you break the law, you may get arrested.*

break a record to destroy a previously set high record by setting a new one. □ *The athlete broke all the school records in swimming.* □ *The record was broken after thirty years.*

break camp to close down a campsite; to pack up and move on. □ *Early this morning, we broke camp and moved northward.* □ *Okay, everyone. It's time to break camp. Take those tents down and fold them neatly.*

break new ground to begin to do something that no one else has done; to pioneer (in an enterprise). □ *Dr. Anderson has broken new ground in cancer research.* □ *They were breaking new ground in consumer electronics.*

break one's back (to do something) See break one's neck (to do something).

break one's habit See break a habit.

break one's neck (to do something) AND **break one's back (to do something)** to work very hard to do something. (Never used in its literal sense.) □ *I broke my neck to get here on time.* □ *That's the last time I'll break my neck to help you.* □ *There is no point in breaking your back. Take your time.*

break one's word not to do what one said one would do; not to keep one's promise. □ *Don't say you'll visit your grandmother if you can't go. She hates for people to break their word.* □ *If you break your word, she won't trust you again.*

break someone's fall to cushion a falling person; to lessen the impact of a falling person. □ *When the little boy fell out of the* *window, the bushes broke his fall.* □ *The old lady slipped on the ice, but a snowbank broke her fall.*

break the bank to leave someone without any money; to exhaust one's source of money. □ *It will hardly break the bank if we go out to dinner just once.* □ *Buying a new dress at that price won't break the bank.*

break the habit See break a habit.

break the law See break a law.

break the news (to someone) to tell someone some important news, usually bad news. □ *The doctor had to break the news to Jane about her husband's cancer.* □ *I hope that the doctor broke the news gently.*

break up (with someone) to end a romantic relationship with someone. □ *Tom broke up with Mary and started dating Lisa.* □ *We broke up in March, after an argument.*

breathe one's last to die. □ *She breathed her last at about two o'clock that afternoon.* □ *Cradled in his wife's arms, he breathed his last.*

brew a plot to plot something; to make a plot. □ *The children brewed a cruel plot to get revenge on their teacher.* □ *We brewed a plot so that we would not have to help with dinner.*

brimming with something 1. [of a container] full of something to the point of overflowing. □ *Tom's glass was brimming with milk.* □ *The pool was brimming with water.* **2.** [of a person] full of some kind of good or happy feeling. □ *The volunteer worker was brimming with goodwill.* □ *The giggling children were brimming with joy.*

bring someone or something up to mention a topic, question, or person's name. □ *Why did you have to bring Bob's name up while I am eating?* □ *I want to bring this matter up for a vote.*

bring someone to justice to punish someone for a crime. □ *The police officer swore she would not rest until she had brought the killer to justice.* □ *Years later, the rapist was finally brought to justice.*

bring the house down to excite a theatrical audience to laughter or applause or both. (Not literal.) □ *This is a great joke. The last* *time I told it, it brought the house down.* T *It didn't bring down the house. It emptied it.*

a **bull in a china shop** a very clumsy person around breakable things; a thoughtless or tactless person. (China is fine crockery.) □ *Get that big dog out of my garden. It's like a bull in a china shop.* □ *Bob is so rude—a regular bull in a china shop.*

burn someone up to anger someone; to make someone mad. □ *Seeing people throw litter on the ground just burns me up.* □ *It burns Jane up when people don't respond to her invitations.*

burst into flame(s) [for something] to catch fire and quickly become a large fire. □ *As soon as a piece of the drapery touched the candle, the entire wall seemed to burst into flames.* □ *The two cars burst into flame soon after the collision.*

burst with joy to be full to the bursting point with happiness. □ *When I got my grades, I could have burst with joy.* □ *Joe was not exactly bursting with joy when he got the news.*

the **business end of something** the part or end of something that actually does the work or carries out the procedure. □ *Keep away from the business end of the electric drill so you don't get hurt.* □ *Don't point the business end of that gun at anyone. It might go off.*

Business is business. We have to carry on with our business even if there are bad results in the process.; Making the business work is more important than making employees happy. □ *I am sorry about having to fire you, but business is business.* □ *Business is business, and we have to make a profit.*

buy something to believe something that someone says; to accept something to be a fact. (Often in the negative. Also used literally.) □ *It may be true, but I don't buy it.* □ *I just don't buy the idea that you can swim that far.* □ *Do you really expect me to buy that story? It's clearly a lie.*

buy something for a song to buy something cheaply. □ *No one else wanted it, so I bought it for a song.* □ *I could buy this house for a song, because it's so ugly.*

Buzz off! Leave here!; Go away! □ *Buzz off! Stop bothering me!* □ *Why don't you just buzz off? Get out!*

by chance accidentally; randomly; without planning. □ *I found this book by chance at a book sale.* □ *We met by chance in a class in college.*

by check by using a check. □ *He paid for the book by check.* □ *You will be paid by check.*

by day AND **by night** during the day; during the night. □ *By day, Mary worked in an office; by night, she took classes.* □ *Dave slept by day and worked by night.*

by dribs and drabs [of something happening] in small, irregular quantities. □ *The checks for the charity are coming in by dribs and drabs.* □ *The members of the orchestra arrived by dribs and drabs.*

by hand made or done by one's hands; made by human hands as opposed to by a machine. □ *This fine wooden cabinet was made by hand.* □ *I carved this figurine by hand.*

by night See by day.

by rote [of learning or memorizing] done as habit and without thinking. □ *I memorized the speech by rote. I don't know what it means.* □ *The student learns everything by rote and can't pass the test.*

by the _____ each; per. (Used to show a unit of measure, but not the rate of measure.) □ *Lettuce is sold by the head.* □ *Gas is sold by the gallon.*

by the way in addition to what I just said; while I think of it; incidentally. □ *By the way, I think your tie is stunning.* □ *By the way, you left the car unlocked when you used it last.*

Call again. Please visit this shop again sometime. (Said by shop-keepers and clerks.) □ *"Thank you," said the clerk, smiling. "Call again."* □ *CLERK: Is that everything? JOHN: Yes. CLERK: That's ten dollars even. JOHN: Here you are. CLERK: Thanks. Call again.*

call a meeting to order to announce that a meeting is about to begin. □ *The president called the meeting to order.* □ *The meeting will be called to order at noon.*

call a spade a spade to call something by its right name; to speak frankly about something, even if it is unpleasant. □ *Well, I believe it's time to call a spade a spade. We are just avoiding the issue.* □ *Let's call a spade a spade. The man is a liar.*

call for someone or something to need, require, or demand something or the services of someone. □ *The recipe calls for two cups of flour.* □ *This job calls for someone with good eyesight.*

call it quits to quit; to resign from something; to announce that one is quitting. □ *Okay! I've had enough! I'm calling it quits.* □ *Time to go home, John. Let's call it quits.*

call of nature the need to go to the toilet. □ *Stop the car here! I have to answer the call of nature.* □ *There was no interval in the meeting to take care of a call of nature.*

call on someone to visit someone. □ *I have to call on my aunt this Sunday.* □ *Bill called on his brother in the hospital.*

call out (to someone) to shout to someone. □ *Mike called out to Tom that there was a telephone call for him.* □ *I heard someone call out, but I could see no one.*

call someone names to call someone by an abusive or insulting name. □ *Billy cried when the other kids called him names.* □ *John was punished for calling his teacher names.*

call (the) roll AND **take (the) roll** to call the names of people on the roll, expecting them to reply if they are present. (*Roll* here refers to a list of people who belong to a certain group or who are expected to be present.) □ *After I call the roll, please open your books to page 12.* □ *I will take roll, and then we will do arithmetic.*

cannot help doing something not able to refrain from doing something; not able not to do something. □ *Anne is such a good cook, I can't help eating everything she makes.* □ *Since John loves to shop, he can't help spending money.*

cannot stomach someone or something See not able to stomach someone or something.

Can't fight city hall. See You can't fight city hall.

can't wait (for something to happen) [to be very eager and] to be unable to endure the wait for something to happen. □ *I am so anxious for my birthday to come. I just can't wait.* □ *Tom can't wait for Mary to arrive.*

can't wait (to do something) [to be very eager and] unable to endure the wait until it is possible to do something. □ *I'm glad it's almost summertime—I just can't wait to go swimming!* □ *Jimmy can't wait to go to school tomorrow.*

Can you top that? Can you do something or tell about something that is better, funnier, or more extreme than that? □ *And then she was rude enough to ask to use my telephone! Can you top that?* □ *I just got a contract for $2,000,000 in sales. Can you top that?*

capable of (doing) something having the ability to do something. □ *Do you think Tom is capable of lifting 200 pounds?* □ *No one I know is capable of such a crime!*

carry a secret to one's grave See carry a secret to the grave.

carry a secret to the grave AND **carry a secret to one's grave** to avoid telling a secret, even to the day of one's death. □ *John carried our secret to his grave.* □ *Trust me, I will carry your secret to the grave!*

case in point an example of what one is talking about. □ *Now, as a case in point, let's look at nineteenth-century England.* □ *Fireworks can be dangerous. For a case in point, look at what happened to Bob Smith last week.*

a **case of mistaken identity** the incorrect identification of someone. □ *It is simply a case of mistaken identity.* □ *I am not the criminal you want to arrest. This is a case of mistaken identity.*

Cash or credit (card)? Do you wish to pay for your purchases with cash or a credit card? □ *Mary put all her packages on the counter. Then the clerk asked, "Cash or credit card?"* □ *CLERK: Is that everything? RACHEL: Yes. That's all. CLERK: Cash or credit?*

cast aspersions on someone to make a rude and insulting remark. □ *I resent your casting aspersions on my brother and his ability!* □ *It is rude to cast aspersions on people in general.*

cast one's vote to vote; to place one's ballot in the ballot box. □ *The citizens cast their votes for president.* □ *The wait in line to cast one's vote was almost an hour.*

catch cold AND **take cold** to contract a cold (the disease). □ *Please close the window, or we'll all catch cold.* □ *I take cold every year at this time.*

catch fire to begin to burn; to ignite. □ *If the wood were not so wet, it would catch fire more easily.* □ *The curtains blew against the flame of the candle and caught fire.*

Catch me later. AND **Catch me some other time.** Please try to talk to me later. □ *BILL (angry): Tom, look at this phone bill! TOM: Catch me later.* □ *"Catch me some other time," hollered Mr. Franklin over his shoulder. "I've got to go to the airport."*

Catch me some other time. See Catch me later.

catch one's breath to struggle for normal breathing after strenuous activity. (Compare with get (enough) time to catch one's breath.) □ *The jogger stopped to catch her breath.* □ *It took Jimmy a minute to catch his breath after being punched in the stomach.*

catch someone's eye 1. to appear and attract someone's interest. □ *A small red car passing by caught my eye.* □ *One of the books on the top shelf caught my eye, and I took it down to look at it.* **2.** to cause someone to notice one; to get someone's attention. □ *I tried to catch Jane's eye so I could talk to her, but she didn't notice me.* □ *He waved, trying to catch my eye, but I didn't recognize him.*

catch wind of something See get wind of something.

child's play something that is performed effortlessly. □ *The exam was child's play to her.* □ *Finding the right street is child's play with a map.*

chisel someone out of something to cheat someone to get money or belongings. □ *The company tried to chisel the government out of taxes it owed.* □ *Bill chiseled his little sister out of her allowance.*

claim a life [for something] to take the life of someone; [for something] to cause someone's death. □ *The killer tornado claimed the lives of six people at the trailer park.* □ *A skiing accident claimed the athlete's life.*

clear of something without touching something; away from something. □ *Please stand clear of the doors while the train is moving.* □ *Make sure the dog moves clear of the driveway before you back the car up.*

clear the table to remove the dishes and other eating utensils from the table after a meal. □ *Will you please help clear the table?* □ *After you clear the table, we'll play cards.*

come across someone or something AND **run across someone or something** to find someone or something; to discover someone or something. □ *John came across a book he had been looking for.* □ *Where did you run across that lovely skirt?*

Come and get it! Dinner is ready! Come and eat it. □ *Everything is ready. Come and get it!* □ *Come and get it! It's getting cold.*

come apart at the seams to lose one's emotional self-control suddenly. (From the literal sense, referring to a garment falling apart.) □ *Bill was so upset that he almost came apart at the seams.* □ *I couldn't take anymore. I just came apart at the seams.*

come away empty-handed to return without anything. (Compare with go away empty-handed.) □ *All right, go gambling. Don't come away empty-handed, though.* □ *Go to the bank and ask for the loan again. This time don't come away empty-handed.*

come down with something AND **be down with something** to become or to be sick with some illness. □ *Susan came down with a bad cold and had to cancel her trip.* □ *I didn't go to work because I was down with the flu.*

come into one's or its own [for someone or something] to achieve the proper recognition. □ *After years of trying, Sally* *finally came into her own as an actress.* □ *When will the idea of an electric car come into its own?*

Come off it! Don't act so arrogant!; Don't try to maintain your air of detachment!; Cut the act!; Don't pretend you don't know what I'm talking about!; Don't pretend you don't know how conceited you look or sound. □ *You are not as successful as you make it seem. Come off it!* □ *You are just a worker like the rest of us. Come off it!*

come out in the wash to work out all right. □ *Don't worry about that problem. It'll all come out in the wash.* □ *This trouble will go away. It'll come out in the wash.*

come out of the closet 1. to reveal one's secret interests. □ *Bob Brown came out of the closet and admitted that he likes to knit.* □ *It's time for all of you lovers of chamber music to come out of the closet and start attending our concerts.* **2.** to reveal that one is a homosexual. □ *Tom surprised his parents when he came out of the closet.* □ *It was difficult for him to come out of the closet.*

come to a dead end to come to an absolute stopping point. □ *The building project came to a dead end.* □ *The street came to a dead end.* □ *We were driving along and came to a dead end.*

come to a head to come to a crucial point; to come to a point when a problem must be solved. □ *Remember my problem with my neighbors? Well, last night the whole thing came to a head.* □ *The battle between the two factions of the city council came to a head yesterday.*

come to a stop [for someone or something] to stop moving or happening. □ *The bus finally came to a stop so I could get off.* □ *The loud noise finally came to a stop.*

come to the point AND **get to the point** to get to the important part (of something). □ *He has been talking a long time. I wish he would come to the point.* □ *Quit wasting time! Get to the point!* □ *We are talking about money, Bob! Come on, get to the point.*

come what may no matter what might happen. □ *I'll be home for the holidays, come what may.* □ *Come what may, the mail will get delivered.*

contrary to something in spite of something; regardless of something. □ *Contrary to what you might think, I am neat and tidy.* □ *Contrary to popular opinion, my uncle is well and healthy.*

control the purse strings to be in charge of the money in a business or a household. □ *I control the purse strings at our house.* □ *Mr. Williams is the treasurer. He controls the purse strings.*

cook something to perfection to cook something perfectly. □ *John cooked my steak to perfection.* □ *The entire dinner was cooked to perfection!*

(Could I) give you a lift? Can I offer you a ride someplace? (Also used with *can* or *may* in place of *could*.) □ *Bill stopped his car at the side of the road near where Tom stood. "Can I give you a lift?" asked Bill.* □ *JOHN: Well, I've got to leave. ALICE: Me, too. JOHN: Give you a lift? ALICE: Sure. Thanks.*

Could I have a lift? AND **How about a lift?** Would you please give me a ride (in your car)? (This usually refers to a destination that is the same as the driver's or on the way to the driver's destination. Also used with *can* or *may* in place of *could*.) □ *BOB: Going north? Could I have a lift? BILL: Sure. Hop in. BOB: Thanks. That's such a long walk to the north end of campus.* □ *SUE: Can I have a lift? I'm late. MARY: Sure, if you're going somewhere on Maple Street.*

Could I join you? AND **(Do you) mind if I join you?** Will you permit me to sit with you? (An inquiry seeking permission to sit at someone's table or join someone else in some activity. Also used with *can* or *may* in place of *could*.) □ *Tom came into the café and saw Fred and Sally sitting in a booth by the window. Going up to them, Tom said, "Could I join you?"* □ *"Do you mind if I join you?" asked the lady. "There are no other seats."*

Could you keep a secret? I am going to tell you something that I hope you will keep a secret. (Also used with *can* in place of *could*.) □ *TOM: Could you keep a secret? MARY: Sure. TOM: Don't tell anybody, but I'm going to be a daddy.* □ *SUE: Can you keep a secret? ALICE: Of course. SUE: We're moving to Atlanta.*

count on someone or something to rely on someone or something; to depend on someone or something. □ *I can count on Bill to get the job done.* □ *Can I count on this car to start every morning of the year?*

a **couple of** _____ two; two or three; a few; some; not many. □ *Bill grabbed a couple of beers from the refrigerator.* □ *I hung a couple of pictures on the wall.*

course of action the procedures or sequence of actions that someone will follow to accomplish a goal. □ *I plan to follow a course of action that will produce the best results.* □ *The committee planned a course of action that would reduce costs and eliminate employees.*

cover a lot of ground 1. to travel over a great distance; to investigate a wide expanse of land. □ *The prospectors covered a lot of ground looking for gold.* □ *My car can cover a lot of ground in one day.* **2.** to deal with much information and many facts. □ *The history lecture covered a lot of ground today.* □ *Mr. and Mrs. Franklin always cover a lot of ground when they argue.*

cover something up to hide the truth about something. □ *The representative tried to cover up her involvement in the scandal.* □ *The memo was a clear attempt to cover up the executive's criminal activities.*

crack a joke to tell a joke. □ *She's never serious. She's always cracking jokes.* □ *As long as she's cracking jokes, she's okay.*

crazy about someone or something very fond of someone or something; very enthusiastic about someone or something. □ *I'm crazy about camping.* □ *Grandpa and Grandma are still crazy about each other.*

a **credit to someone or something** someone or something that makes someone proud; someone or something that is worthy of honor. □ *John, the chemist, is a credit to his discipline.* □ *Well-behaved children are a credit to their parents.*

cross swords (with someone) to enter into an argument with someone. (Not literal.) □ *I don't want to cross swords with Tom.* □ *The last time we crossed swords, we had a terrible time.*

the **crux of the matter** the central issue of the matter. (*Crux* is an old word meaning "cross.") □ *All right, this is the crux of the matter.* □ *It's about time we looked at the crux of the matter.*

cry bloody murder See scream bloody murder.

curl up and die to retreat and die. □ *When I heard you say that, I could have curled up and died.* □ *No, it wasn't an illness. She just curled up and died.*

curry favor with someone to try to get special favor from someone. □ *They tried to curry favor with the professor by working hard.* □ *Bill could never curry favor with the boss, but he kept trying.*

cut class See cut school.

Cut it out! Stop doing that!; Stop saying that! (Colloquial and familiar.) □ *SUE: Why, I think you have a crush on Mary! TOM: Cut it out!* □ *"Cut it out!" yelled Tommy as Billy hit him again.*

cut school AND **cut class** to fail to attend a class or a day of school. □ *As a joke, one day all the students cut their math class and went to lunch instead.* □ *Jane was punished by her parents after she cut school.*

cut someone off (short) to interrupt someone who is speaking. □ *Bob cut her off short and wouldn't let her finish talking.* □ *Please don't cut me off in the middle of a sentence!*

Cut the comedy! AND **Cut the funny stuff!** Stop acting silly and telling jokes!; Be serious! □ *JOHN: All right, you guys! Cut the comedy and get to work! BILL: Can't we ever have any fun? JOHN: No.* □ *BILL: Come on, Mary, let's throw Tom in the pool! MARY: Yeah, let's drag him over and give him a good dunking! TOM: Okay, you clowns, cut the funny stuff! I'll throw both of you in! BILL: You and what army?*

Cut the funny stuff! See Cut the comedy!

cut the ground out from under someone to destroy the foundation of someone's plans or someone's argument. □ *The politician cut the ground out from under his opponent.* □ *Congress cut the ground out from under the president.*

dart in and out [for something moving] to move quickly between two things, or into a number of things, and move away again. □ *On the highway, a small car was darting in and out of the two right lanes of traffic.* □ *A small bird darted in and out of the bush, probably going to a nest inside.*

date back (to some time) to extend back to a particular time; to have been alive at a particular time in the past. □ *The old house dates back to the Civil War.* □ *This phonograph record dates back to the sixties.* □ *My older brothers were born in the 1940s, but I don't date back that far.*

dawn on someone to occur to someone; to become clearly understood. □ *Suddenly, it dawned on me that I was late for work.* □ *It finally dawned on the inspector that John had stolen the money.*

days running AND **weeks running; months running; years running** days in a series; months in a series; etc. (Follows a number.) □ *I had a bad cold for five days running.* □ *For two years running, I brought work home from the office every night.*

dead and buried gone forever. (Refers literally to persons and figuratively to ideas and other things.) □ *Now that Uncle Bill is dead and buried, we can read his will.* □ *That kind of thinking is dead and buried.*

the **death of someone** the end of someone; the cause of someone's death. (Rarely literal.) □ *This job will be the death of me!* □ *Jane thought the long trip would be the death of her.*

death on someone or something 1. very effective in acting against someone or something. □ *This road is terribly bumpy. It's death on tires.* □ *The sergeant is death on lazy soldiers.* **2.** [with *something*] accurate or deadly at doing something requiring skill or great effort. □ *John is death on curve balls. He's our best pitcher.* □ *The boxing champ is really death on those fast punches.*

deem it (to be) necessary AND **deem that it is necessary** to believe that something is necessary. □ *Mary deemed that it was necessary to leave town that night.* □ *Lisa deemed it necessary to go home.*

deem that it is necessary See deem it (to be) necessary.

den of iniquity a place filled with wickedness. □ *The town was a den of iniquity and vice was everywhere.* □ *Police raided the gambling house, calling it a den of iniquity.*

depart (this life) to die. (A euphemism.) □ *He departed this life on April 20, 1973.* □ *She departed peacefully, in her sleep.*

desert a sinking ship AND **leave a sinking ship** to leave a place, a person, or a situation when things become difficult or unpleasant. (Rats are said to be the first to leave a ship that is sinking.) □ *I hate to be the one to desert a sinking ship, but I can't stand it around here anymore.* □ *There goes Tom. Wouldn't you know he'd leave a sinking ship rather than stay around and try to help?*

die by one's own hand to commit suicide. □ *JANE: I just heard that Bill died. I didn't know he was sick. DAN: He wasn't sick. He died by his own hand.* □ *She died at the age of fifty, by her own hand.*

die of boredom to suffer from boredom; to be very bored. □ *No one has ever really died of boredom.* □ *We sat there and listened politely, even though we almost died of boredom.*

die on the vine [for something] to decline or fade away at an early stage of development. (Also used literally in reference to grapes or other fruit.) □ *You have a great plan, Tom. Let's keep it alive. Don't let it die on the vine.* □ *The whole project died on the vine when the contract was canceled.*

Dig in! Please start eating your meal (heartily). □ *When we were all seated at the table, Grandfather said, "Dig in!" and we all did.* □ *SUE: Sit down, everybody. BOB: Wow, this stuff looks good! ALICE: It sure does. SUE: Dig in!*

dig up some dirt on someone to find out something bad about someone. (This dirt is gossip.) □ *The citizens' group dug up some dirt on the mayor and used it against her at election time.* ⊤ *If you don't stop trying to dig some dirt up on me, I'll get a lawyer and sue you.*

divert something into something to steal something and keep it someplace. □ *He diverted the funds into a secret bank account.* □ *She diverted her clients' stock purchases into her own investment portfolio.*

Does it work for you? Is this all right with you?; Do you agree? (Colloquial. Can be answered by "(It) works for me.") □ *BILL: I'll be there at noon. Does it work for you? BOB: Works for me.* □ *MARY: We're having dinner at eight. Does it work for you? JANE: Sounds just fine.*

Do I have to paint (you) a picture? See Do I have to spell it out (for you)?

Do I have to spell it out (for you)? AND **Do I have to paint (you) a picture?** What do I have to do to make this clear enough for you to understand? (Shows impatience.) □ *MARY: I don't think I understand what you're trying to tell me, Fred. FRED: Do I have to spell it out for you? MARY: I guess so. FRED: We're through, Mary.* □ *SALLY: Would you please go over the part about the square root again? MARY: Do I have to paint you a picture? Pay attention!*

Don't believe I've had the pleasure. See I don't believe I've had the pleasure.

Don't breathe a word of this to anyone. This is a secret or secret gossip. Do not tell it to anyone. □ *MARY: Can you keep a secret? JOHN: Sure. MARY: Don't breathe a word of this to anyone, but Tom is in jail.* □ *BILL: Have you heard about Mary and her friends? SALLY: No. Tell me! Tell me! BILL: Well, they all secretly went to Mexico for the weekend. Everyone thinks they are at Mary's, except Mary's mother, who thinks they are at Sue's. Now, don't breathe a word of this to anyone. SALLY: Of course not! You know me!*

Don't call us, we'll call you. Don't bother to try to find out if you were selected by calling us. Instead, if we select you, we will call you. (Usually this means that no one will call.) □ *Thank you for auditioning for the part in the play. Don't call us, we'll call you.* □ *I will file your application. Don't call us, we'll call you.*

Don't get me wrong. Please don't misunderstand me.; Please don't think that I am being entirely negative. □ *Don't get me wrong. I think you are doing good work, but some improvements can be made.* □ *Don't get me wrong. I really like you.*

Don't get up. Please, there is no need to rise to greet me or in deference to me. (Often with *please*.) □ *Mary approached the table to speak to Bill. Bill started to push his chair back as if to rise. Mary said, "Don't get up. I just want to say hello."* □ *TOM (rising): Hello, Fred. Good to see you. FRED (standing): Don't get up. How are you?*

Don't get your bowels in an uproar! Do not get so excited! (Slang.) □ *BILL: What have you done to my car? Where's the bumper? The side window is cracked! BOB: Calm down! Don't get your bowels in an uproar!* □ *FATHER: Now, son, we need to talk a little bit about you and your pet snake. Where is it? JOHN: I don't know. FATHER (outraged): What! JOHN: Don't get your bowels in an uproar! It always turns up.*

Don't give it another thought. See Think nothing of it.

Don't give it a (second) thought. See Think nothing of it.

Don't give me that! Don't say those things!; Don't make those excuses to me.; Don't whine and complain to me. □ *Don't give me that! Do what I told you to do!* □ *One excuse after another! Don't give me that!*

Don't give up! Do not stop trying!; Keep trying! □ *JOHN: Get in there and give it another try. Don't give up! BILL: Okay. Okay. But it's hopeless.* □ *JANE: I asked the boss for a raise, but he said no. TOM: Don't give up. Try again later.*

Don't give up the ship! Do not give up yet!; Do not yield the entire enterprise! (From a naval expression.) □ *BILL: I'm having a devil of a time with calculus. I think I want to drop the course. SALLY: Keep trying. Don't give up the ship!* □ *BILL: Every time we get enough money saved up to make a down payment on a house, the price of houses skyrockets. I'm about ready to stop trying. SUE: We'll manage. Don't give up the ship!*

Don't give up too eas(il)y! AND **Don't give up without a fight!** Do not yield so easily.; Keep struggling and you may win.; Do not give up too soon. □ *SUE: She says no every time I ask her for a raise. MARY: Well, don't give up too easily. Keep after her.* □ *JOHN: I know it's my discovery, not hers, but she won't admit it. SALLY: Don't give up without a fight.*

Don't give up without a fight! See Don't give up too eas(il)y!

Don't hold your breath. Do not stop breathing while you are waiting for something to happen. (Meaning that it will take longer for it to happen than you can possibly hold your breath.) □ *TOM: The front yard is such a mess. BOB: Bill's supposed to rake the leaves. TOM: Don't hold your breath. He never does his share of the work.* □ *SALLY: Someone said that gasoline prices would go down. BOB: Oh, yeah? Don't hold your breath.*

Don't I know you from somewhere? a way of striking up a conversation with a stranger, probably at a party or other gathering. □ *BILL: Don't I know you from somewhere? MARY: I don't think so. Where did you go to school?* □ *HENRY: Don't I know you from somewhere? ALICE: No, and let's keep it that way.*

Don't make me laugh! Do not make such ridiculous statements— they only make me laugh. □ *MARY: I'll be a millionaire by the time I'm thirty. TOM: Don't make me laugh! MARY: I will! I will!* □ *MARY: I'm trying out for cheerleader. SUE: You, a cheerleader? Don't make me laugh!*

Don't push (me)! Don't put pressure on me to do something! (Also literal.) □ *SUE: You really must go to the dentist, you know. JOHN: Don't push me. I'll go when I'm good and ready.* □ *BOB: Come on! You can finish. Keep trying. BILL: Don't push me! I have to do it under my own steam!*

Don't stand on ceremony. Do not wait for a formal invitation.; Please be at ease and make yourself at home. (Some people read this as "Don't remain standing because of ceremony," and others read it as "Don't be totally obedient to the requirements of ceremony.") □ *JOHN: Come in, Tom. Don't stand on ceremony. Get yourself a drink and something to eat and mingle with the other guests. TOM: Okay, but I can only stay for a few minutes.* □ *"Don't stand on ceremony, Fred," urged Sally. "Go around and introduce yourself to everyone."*

Don't sweat it! Don't worry about it. (Slang.) □ *BILL: I think I'm flunking algebra! BOB: Don't sweat it! Everybody's having a rough time.* □ *MARY: Good grief! I just stepped on the cat's tail, but I guess you heard. SUE: Don't sweat it! The cat's got to learn to keep out of the way.*

Don't tell a soul. Please do not tell anyone this gossip. □ *BILL: Is your brother getting married? SALLY: Yes, but don't tell a soul. It's* *a secret.* □ *MARY: Can you keep a secret? JOHN: Sure. MARY: Don't tell a soul, but Tom is in jail.*

Don't waste your breath. You will not get a positive response to what you have to say, so don't even say it.; Talking will get you nowhere. □ *ALICE: I'll go in there and try to convince her otherwise. FRED: Don't waste your breath. I already tried it.* □ *SALLY: No, I won't agree! Don't waste your breath. BILL: Aw, come on.*

Don't waste your time. You will not get anywhere with it, so don't waste time trying. □ *MARY: Should I ask Tom if he wants to go to the convention, or is he still in a bad mood? SALLY: Don't waste your time. MARY: Bad mood, huh?* □ *JANE: I'm having trouble fixing this doorknob. MARY: Don't waste your time. I've ordered a new one.*

Don't you dare! You must not do or say that!; Do not even try to do or say that! □ *You are going to tell my friend about what I did? Don't you dare!* □ *You can't say that to her! Don't you dare!*

do someone a kindness to do a kind deed for a person. □ *My neighbor did me a kindness when he cut my grass.* □ *I am always happy to have the opportunity of doing someone a kindness.*

do someone's bidding to do what is requested. □ *The servant grumbled but did his employer's bidding.* □ *Am I expected to do your bidding whenever you ask?*

do something for a living to do some kind of work to earn enough money to live. □ *John paints houses for a living.* □ *What do you do for a living?*

do something in a heartbeat to do something almost immediately. □ *If I had the money, I would go back to college in a heartbeat.* □ *Just tell me that you need me and I'll be there in a heartbeat.*

do something to excess to do too much of something; to consume too much of something. □ *Anne often drinks to excess at parties.* □ *John smokes to excess when he works.*

do the dishes to wash the dishes; to wash and dry the dishes. □ *Bill, you cannot go out and play until you've done the dishes.* □ *Why am I always the one who has to do the dishes?*

do without See go without.

down by some amount having a score that is lower, by the specified amount, than someone else's score or the other team's score. □ *At halftime, the home team was down by 14 points.* □ *Down by one run, the team scored two runs in the ninth inning and won the game.*

Do you follow? Do you understand what I am saying?; Do you understand my explanation? □ *MARY: Keep to the right past the fork in the road, and then turn right at the crossroads. Do you follow? JANE: No. Run it by me again.* □ *JOHN: Take a large bowl and break two eggs into it and beat them. Do you follow? SUE: Sure.*

Do you mind? 1. You are intruding on my space!; You are offending me! (Impatient or incensed. Essentially, "Do you mind stopping what you are doing?") □ *The lady behind her in line kept pushing against her every time the line moved. Finally, Sue turned and said sternly, "Do you mind?"* □ *All through the first part of the movie, two people in the row behind John kept up a running conversation. Finally, as their talking grew loud enough to cause a number of people to say "Shhh," John rose and turned, leaned over into their faces, and shouted, "Do you mind?"* **2.** Do you object to what was suggested or what I am poised to do? □ *Mary had her hand on the lovely silver cake knife that would carry the very last piece of cake to her plate. She looked at Tom, who stood next to her, eyeing the cake. "Do you mind?" she asked coyly.* □ *"Do you mind?" asked Sally, reaching for the phone that Bill was about to use. "I have to call the hospital."*

(Do you) mind if I join you? See Could I join you?

draw blood 1. to hit or bite (a person or an animal), causing a wound that bleeds. □ *The dog chased me and bit me hard, but it didn't draw blood.* □ *The boxer landed just one punch and drew blood immediately.* **2.** to anger or insult a person. □ *Sally screamed out a terrible insult at Tom. Judging by the look on his face, she really drew blood.* □ *Tom started yelling and cursing, trying to insult Sally. He wouldn't be satisfied until he had drawn blood, too.*

draw lots to choose from a group of things to determine who will do something. (Typically, to choose a straw from a bundle of straws. The person with the shortest straw is selected.) □ *We* *drew lots to decide who would wash the dishes.* □ *The players drew lots to determine who would go first.*

a **dream come true** a wish or a dream that has become real. □ *Going to Hawaii is like having a dream come true.* □ *Having you for a friend is a dream come true.*

drive one out of one's mind See drive someone crazy.

drive someone crazy AND **drive someone insane; drive one out of one's mind** to force someone into a state. □ *The sound of the wind howling drove me crazy.* □ *The dog's constant barking drove me insane.*

drive someone insane See drive someone crazy.

drop names to mention the names of important or famous people as if they were personal friends. □ *Mary always tries to impress people by dropping the names of well-known film stars.* □ *Bill's such a snob. Leave it to him to drop the names of all the local gentry.*

drop someone a line to send someone a message, note, or letter. □ *Please drop me a line when you reach London.* □ *I try to drop my aunt a line every month.*

drop the ball to make a blunder; to fail in some way. (Also used literally, in sports: to drop a ball in error.) □ *Everything was going fine in the election until my campaign manager dropped the ball.* □ *You can't trust John to do the job right. He's always dropping the ball.*

drop the other shoe to do the deed that completes something; to do the expected remaining part of something. (Refers to the removal of shoes at bedtime. One shoe is dropped, and then the process is completed when the second shoe drops.) □ *Mr. Franklin has left his wife. Soon he'll drop the other shoe and divorce her.* □ *Tommy has just failed three classes in school. We expect him to drop the other shoe and quit altogether any day now.*

Dry up! Be quiet!; Stop talking so much!; Stop saying things I don't want to hear. □ *Quiet! Dry up! You talk too much.* □ *Just dry up! You have nothing to say.*

earn one's keep to help out with chores in return for food and a place to live; to earn one's pay by doing what is expected. □ *I earn my keep at college by shoveling snow in the winter.* □ *Tom hardly earns his keep around here. He should be fired.*

easy come, easy go said to explain the loss of something that required only a small amount of effort to get in the first place. □ *Anne found twenty dollars in the morning and spent it foolishly at noon. "Easy come, easy go," she said.* □ *John spends his money as fast as he can earn it. With John it's easy come, easy go.*

eat one's heart out 1. to be very sad (about someone or something). □ *Bill spent a lot of time eating his heart out after his divorce.* □ *Sally ate her heart out when she had to sell her house.* **2.** to be envious (of someone or something). □ *Do you like my new watch? Well, eat your heart out. It was the last one in the store.* □ *Don't eat your heart out about my new car. Go get one of your own.*

an **end in itself** for its own sake; toward its own ends; toward no purpose but its own. □ *For Bob, art is an end in itself. He doesn't hope to make any money from it.* □ *Learning is an end in itself. Knowledge does not have to have a practical application.*

end it (all) to kill oneself. □ *He had been depressed for months. He decided to end it all.* □ *I'm no good to anybody. I'm going to end it. Don't try to talk me out of it.*

Enough of that! Stop that!; No more of that behavior! □ *Stop it! Enough of that!* □ *Boys, stop fighting. Enough of that!*

Enough said. No more needs to be said.; I have said all that needs to be said on that matter. □ *I don't want you to make this error again. Enough said.* □ *Enough said. Let's get back to work.*

the **evening of life** old age. □ *As she approached the evening of life, Sarah looked back on her accomplishments with satisfaction.* □ *The residents of this rest home are all in the evening of life.*

every other person or thing every second person or thing; alternating. □ *The magician turned every other card over.* □ *Every other table had an ashtray on it.*

everything but the kitchen sink almost everything one can think of. □ *When Sally went off to college, she took everything but the kitchen sink.* □ *John orders everything but the kitchen sink when he goes out to dinner, especially if someone else is paying for it.*

everything from A to Z See everything from soup to nuts.

everything from soup to nuts AND **everything from A to Z** almost everything one can think of. (The main entry is used especially when describing the many things served at a meal.) □ *For dinner, we had everything from soup to nuts.* □ *In college, I studied everything from soup to nuts.* □ *She mentioned everything from A to Z.*

everything humanly possible everything that is in the range of human powers. □ *The rescuers did everything humanly possible to find the lost campers.* □ *The doctor tried everything humanly possible to save the patient.*

excuse someone from something to free someone from a duty or obligation. □ *Dad excused me from cutting the grass on Saturday.* □ *The teacher excused Susan from taking the quiz because she was ill.*

expecting (a child) pregnant. (A euphemism.) □ *Tommy's mother is expecting a child.* □ *Oh, I didn't know she was expecting.*

Expect me when you see me (coming). I will arrive sometime, but I am not certain when, so when you can actually see me, that's when you'll know I'm arriving. (Jocular and vague.) □ *I don't know what time my train gets in. Expect me when you see me coming.* □ *I'll be there in the morning. Expect me when you see me.*

extend credit (to someone) to grant someone credit. □ *The bank would not extend me any credit, because I have a poor credit record.* □ *The grocery store used to extend credit, but it stopped doing that a few years ago.*

eyeball-to-eyeball person-to-person; face-to-face. □ *The discussions will have to be eyeball-to-eyeball to be effective.* □ *Telephone conversations are a waste of time. We need to talk eyeball-to-eyeball.*

eye of the storm the center of a problem; the center of a commotion or a disturbance. □ *Tom, finding himself at the eye of the storm, tried to blame someone else for the problem.* □ *The manager's office was known as the eye of the storm, since all the major problems ended up there.*

face the music to receive punishment; to accept the unpleasant results of one's actions. □ *Mary broke the kitchen window and had to face the music when her father got home.* □ *After failing a math test, Tom had to go home and face the music.*

fair-haired boy a favored person. (Not necessarily young or a boy.) □ *The teacher's fair-haired boy always does well on tests.* □ *The supervisor's son was the fair-haired boy on the construction site.*

fall apart to break into pieces; to become disconnected; to break into parts. □ *My old car is about ready to fall apart.* □ *The old book fell apart as soon as I opened it.*

fall asleep to go to sleep. □ *I fell asleep while reading the very dull book.* □ *I got in bed and fell asleep at once.*

fall between two stools to come somewhere between two possibilities and fail to meet the requirements of either. □ *The material is not suitable for an academic book, and it is not suitable for a popular one either. It falls between two stools.* □ *He tries to be both teacher and friend, but falls between two stools.*

fall ill to become ill. □ *Tom fell ill just before he was to perform.* □ *We both fell ill after eating the baked fish.*

fall in love [for two people] to recognize and experience love for one another. □ *Bob and Lisa fell in love on a warm day in October.* □ *Anne has fallen in love with various guys a number of times.*

fall to someone to become the responsibility of someone. □ *It always falls to me to apologize first.* □ *Why does it fall to me to answer the telephone every time it rings?*

familiar with someone or something having a good knowledge of someone or something. □ *Are you familiar with changing a flat tire?* □ *I'm can't speak German fluently, but I'm somewhat familiar with the language.*

Fancy meeting you here! I am very surprised to meet you here! (A catchphrase.) □ *TOM: Hi, Sue! Fancy meeting you here! SUE: Hi, Tom. I was thinking the same thing about you.* □ *"Fancy meeting you here," said Mr. Franklin when he bumped into Mrs. Franklin at the racetrack.*

a **fan of someone** to be a follower of someone; to idolize someone. (This word *fan* is from *fanatic* [follower].) □ *My mother is still a fan of the Beatles.* □ *I'm a great fan of the mayor of the town.*

far as I know See as far as I know.

far as I'm concerned See as far as I'm concerned.

far-away look AND **far-off look** an appearance on one's face of having one's mind in another place. □ *Dave had a far-away look in his eyes, so I touched him to get his attention.* □ *Lisa's face had a far-off look, indicating that she was daydreaming.*

far from it on the contrary; that is not at all the case; quite the opposite is true. □ *Did I have a bad day? Far from it. It was great.* □ *We did not win the game. Far from it. We lost by eighteen points.*

far-off look See far-away look.

faster and faster at an increasing rate of speed; fast and then even faster. □ *The car went faster and faster, and I was afraid we would crash.* □ *The cost of education goes up faster and faster every year.*

favor someone or something with something to provide someone or something with something beneficial or special. □ *Mary favored us with a song.* □ *Nature favored Bill with curly hair.*

feast one's eyes (on someone or something) to look at someone or something with pleasure, envy, or admiration. (As if such visions provided a feast of visual delight for one's eyes.) □ *Just feast your eyes on that beautiful, juicy steak!* □ *Yes, feast your eyes. You won't see one like that again for a long time.*

a **feather in one's cap** an honor; a reward for something. □ *Getting a new client was really a feather in my cap.* □ *John earned a feather in his cap by getting an A in physics.*

feel a glow of something a feeling of contentment, happiness, satisfaction, peace, etc. □ *Anne felt a glow of happiness as she held her new baby.* □ *Sitting by the lake, the lovers felt a warm glow of contentment.*

feel guilty (about something) to feel that one is to blame for something; to feel intense regret for something that one has done. □ *I feel guilty for forgetting about your birthday.* □ *You shouldn't feel guilty about the accident. It's not your fault.*

feel like a million (dollars) to feel well and healthy, both physically and mentally. (To feel like something unbelievably good.) □ *A quick swim in the morning makes me feel like a million dollars.* □ *What a beautiful day! It makes you feel like a million.*

feel like doing something to want to do something; to be in the mood to do something. □ *Do you feel like stopping work to eat something?* □ *I feel like going on a vacation.*

feel like something 1. to have the feeling of being something, usually something bad. □ *I said something really stupid and I feel like a fool.* □ *Lisa says she feels like a failure.* **2.** to want to have something, such as food or drink. □ *I really feel like a cold drink right now.* □ *Do you feel like a hamburger?*

feel one's gorge rise to sense that one is getting very angry. □ *I felt my gorge rise, and I knew I was going to lose my temper.* □ *Bob could feel his gorge rise as he read his tax bill.*

feel something in one's bones AND **know something in one's bones** to sense something; to have an intuition about something. □ *The train will be late. I feel it in my bones.* □ *I failed the test. I know it in my bones.*

fend for oneself to take care of oneself. □ *My parents went on vacation, leaving me to fend for myself.* □ *Since you're 18, you're old enough to fend for yourself.*

fiddle (around) with something to play aimlessly with something; to meddle with something. □ *Stop fiddling with the light switch!* □ *Bill fiddled around with the vase until he dropped it.*

field questions to answer a series of questions, especially from reporters. □ *After her speech, Jane fielded questions from reporters.* □ *The president's press agents fielded questions from the newspaper.*

a **fighting chance** a good possibility of success, especially if every effort is made. □ *They have at least a fighting chance of winning the race.* □ *The patient could die, but he has a fighting chance since the operation.*

figure in something to play a role in something; to be a part of something. □ *How does this point figure in your argument?* □ *Your medical expenses will figure in the settlement amount.*

figure on something to plan on something. □ *I figured on arriving at the party around eight o'clock.* □ *Jane figured on spending $25 on dinner.*

find fault with someone or something to seek to find something wrong with someone or something. □ *My father is always finding fault with everything I do.* □ *I was unable to find fault with the car, so I bought it.*

find one's feet to become used to a new situation or experience. □ *She was lonely when she first left home, but she is finding her feet now.* □ *It takes time to learn the office routine, but you will gradually find your feet.*

find someone guilty AND **find someone innocent** to decide guilt or innocence and deliver a verdict in a court of law. □ *The judge found the defendant not guilty by reason of insanity.* □ *The jury found the defendant innocent.*

find someone innocent See find someone guilty.

a **fine kettle of fish** a real mess; an unsatisfactory situation. □ *The dog has eaten the steak we were going to have for dinner. This is a fine kettle of fish!* □ *This is a fine kettle of fish. It's below freezing outside, and the furnace won't work.*

fire a gun to shoot a gun; to discharge a gun. □ *The police caught the robber who had fired the gun.* □ *Jane fired the gun and hit the target.*

Fire away! Begin to do something. (Often refers to speaking or asking questions.) □ *Fire away! I'm ready to take dictation.* □ *If you want me to hear your complaints, fire away!*

First come, first served. The first people to arrive will be served first. (A cliché.) □ *They ran out of tickets before we got there. It was first come, first served, but we didn't know that.* □ *Please line up and take your turn. It's first come, first served.*

first of all the very first thing; before anything else. □ *First of all, put your name on this piece of paper.* □ *First of all, we'll try to find a place to live.*

fish for a compliment to try to get someone to pay oneself a compliment. □ *When she showed me her new dress, I could tell that she was fishing for a compliment.* □ *Tom was certainly fishing for a compliment when he modeled his stylish haircut for his friends.*

fit in with someone or something to belong; to seem to be part of. □ *Anne felt like she didn't fit in with the other students.* □ *Bob's teaching style didn't fit in with that of the other professors at the college.*

fit like a glove to fit very well; to fit tightly or snugly. □ *My new shoes fit like a glove.* □ *My new coat is a little tight. It fits like a glove.*

flatter one's figure to make one look thin. □ *The princess lines of this dress really flatter your figure.* □ *The trousers had a full cut that flattered Maria's figure.*

Flattery will get you nowhere. You can praise me, but I'm not going to give you what you want. □ *I am glad to hear that I am beautiful and talented, but flattery will get you nowhere.* □ *Flattery will get you nowhere, but that doesn't mean you should stop flattering me!*

flirt with the idea of doing something to think about doing something; to toy with an idea; to consider something, but not too seriously. □ *I flirted with the idea of going to Europe for two weeks.* □ *Jane flirted with the idea of quitting her job.*

foist something (off) on someone to force a person to take or do something that the person doesn't want to take or do. □ *Bill tried to foist the task of washing dishes off on his sister.* □ *The city council foisted the new garbage dump on the poorest neighborhood in the city.*

follow one's heart to act according to one's feelings; to obey one's sympathetic or compassionate inclinations. □ *I couldn't decide what to do, so I just followed my heart.* □ *I trust that you will follow your heart in this matter.*

follow one's nose 1. to head straight in the direction that your face is pointing. □ *The Smiths' farm is straight ahead. Just follow your nose.* □ *Follow your nose down the path. You can't miss seeing the cottage.* **2.** to seek the source of a smell; to go to the source of a smell. □ *Just follow your nose to the kitchen, and maybe*

Grandma will cut you a piece of pie. □ *Do you want to see where the pigs are kept? Just follow your nose!*

follow someone's lead to act according to someone else's leadership, guidance, or direction. □ *Just follow my lead and you will not get lost.* □ *John followed his father's lead and became a lawyer.*

follow up (on something) to check (on something) and do what needs to be done. □ *I will follow up on this matter and make sure it is settled.* □ *There is a problem with the bank account. Will you please follow up?*

food for thought something to think about. □ *I don't like your idea very much, but it's food for thought.* □ *Your lecture was very good. It contained much food for thought.*

a **fool's paradise** a condition of apparent happiness that is based on false assumptions and will not last. □ *They think they can live on love alone, but they are in a fool's paradise.* □ *The inhabitants of the island feel politically secure, but they are living in a fool's paradise. They could be invaded at any time.*

foot the bill to pay the bill; to be the one who pays for something. □ *Let's go out and eat. I'll foot the bill.* □ *If the bank goes broke, don't worry. The government will foot the bill.*

for a lark AND **on a lark** for a joke; as something done for fun. □ *For a lark, I wore a clown's wig to school.* □ *On a lark, I skipped school and drove to the beach.*

for all I know . . . I really don't have any idea, so it is even possible that . . . □ *I don't know why John is late. For all I know his plane might never have taken off.* □ *For all I know, the company has already been sold.*

for all the good that will do you although the course of action you propose will probably not benefit you at all. □ *You can report the error to the tax agent, for all the good that will do you.* □ *You can come early if you wish, for all the good that will do you.*

foregone conclusion a conclusion that has already been reached; an inevitable result. □ *That the company was moving to California was a foregone conclusion.* □ *That the mayor will win reelection is a foregone conclusion.*

for free for no charge or cost; free of any cost. □ *They let us into the movie for free.* □ *I will let you have a sample of the candy for free.*

Forget it! Don't spend any more time on this matter.; This is not important.; I cancel my request.; Never mind. □ *It doesn't matter. Forget it!* □ *Forget it! I don't want to waste any more time.*

for instance for example. □ *I've lived in many cities—for instance, Boston, Chicago, and Detroit.* □ *Jane is very generous. For instance, she volunteers her time and gives money to charities.*

for life for the remainder of one's life. □ *The accident caused me to become blind for life.* □ *She will stay in prison for life.*

form an opinion to think up or decide on an opinion. (Note the variations in the examples.) □ *I don't know enough about the issue to form an opinion.* □ *Don't tell me how to think! I can form my own opinion.* □ *I don't form opinions without careful consideration.*

for miles [continuing or extending] along or over a distance of two or more miles. □ *The huge field of wheat extends for miles.* □ *We traveled for miles without stopping.*

for safekeeping for the purpose of keeping someone or something safe. □ *I put my jewelry in the vault for safekeeping.* □ *I checked my fur coat at the entrance to the bar for safekeeping.*

for sale available to be sold. □ *Are the paintings on the wall for sale, or are they just the store's?* □ *Susan told me that her vintage car was not for sale.*

for short as an abbreviation. □ *The Internal Revenue Service is known as the IRS for short.* □ *David goes by Dave for short.*

for someone's or something's sake AND **for the sake of someone or something** for the purpose or benefit of someone or something; to satisfy the demands of someone or something. □ *I made a meatless dinner for John's sake.* □ *The teacher repeated the assignment for the sake of the slower students.*

for the duration for the whole time that something continues; for the entire period of time required for something to be completed; for as long as something takes. □ *We are in this war for the duration.* □ *However long it takes, we'll wait. We are here for the duration.*

for the good of someone or something for the benefit, profit, or advantage of someone or something. □ *The president said the strict drug laws were for the good of the country.* □ *David took a second job for the good of his family.*

for the sake of someone or something See for someone's or something's sake.

fraught with danger [of something] full of something dangerous or unpleasant. □ *The spy's trip to Russia was fraught with danger.* □ *My escape from the kidnappers was fraught with danger.*

free and easy casual. □ *John is so free and easy. How can anyone be so relaxed?* □ *Now, take it easy. Just act free and easy. No one will know you're nervous.*

free gift something extra given to a customer when the customer buys something else. □ *When you order your magazine subscription, this book is yours to keep as our free gift.* □ *This canvas tote is a free gift for everyone who opens an account at our bank today!*

free translation a translation that is not completely accurate and not well thought out. □ *John gave a free translation of the sentence, which did not help us at all.* □ *Anne gave a very free translation of the poem.*

from dawn to dusk during the period of the day when there is light; from the rising of the sun to the setting of the sun. □ *I have to work from dawn to dusk on the farm.* □ *The factory runs from dawn to dusk to produce hats and gloves.*

from hand to hand from one person to a series of other persons; passed from one hand to another. □ *The book traveled from hand to hand until it got back to its owner.* □ *The baby didn't like being passed from hand to hand and soon began crying.*

from Missouri from a place where proof is always needed; accustomed to having proof. (Related to the nickname of the state of Missouri, the Show Me State.) □ *You'll have to prove it to me. I'm from Missouri.* □ *She's from Missouri and has to be shown.*

from overseas from a location on the other side of the Atlantic or Pacific Ocean, according to the point of view of someone located in the U.S. □ *The latest word from overseas is that the treaty has been signed.* □ *Is there any news from overseas about the war?*

from side to side moving first to one side and then to the other, repeatedly. □ *The pendulum of the clock swings from side to side.* □ *The singers swayed from side to side as they sang.*

from start to finish from the beginning to the end; throughout. □ *I disliked the whole business from start to finish.* □ *Mary caused problems from start to finish.*

from the bottom of one's heart sincerely. □ *When I returned the lost kitten to Mrs. Brown, she thanked me from the bottom of her heart.* □ *Oh, thank you! I'm grateful from the bottom of my heart.*

from the other side of the tracks from the poorer part of a town, often near the railroad tracks. □ *Who cares if she's from the other side of the tracks?* □ *I belong to a poor family—we come from the other side of the tracks.*

from the outset throughout, from the very beginning. □ *I felt from the outset that Lisa was the wrong one for the job.* □ *From the outset, I felt unwelcome in the group.*

from the top from the beginning of something, such as a song or a script. □ *Okay, let's try it again from the top.* □ *Play it from the top one more time.*

from the word go from the beginning; from the very start of things. (Actually from the uttering of the word *go*, as at the start of a race.) □ *I knew about the problem from the word go.* □ *She was failing the class from the word go.*

from time to time irregularly; now and then; occasionally; sometimes; not predictably. □ *From time to time, I like to go fishing instead of going to work.* □ *Bob visits us at our house from time to time.*

the **fruit(s) of one's labor(s)** the results of one's work. □ *We displayed the fruits of our labor at the convention.* □ *What have you accomplished? Where is the fruit of your labors?*

full blast See at full blast.

gang up on someone [for a group] to attack [someone]. □ *The thugs ganged up on the tourists and robbed them.* □ *The two bullies ganged up on Max and tried to beat him up.*

gear (oneself) up for something to prepare for something. □ *The citizens on the coast geared up for the approaching hurricane.* □ *I geared up for the big presentation by eating a big breakfast.*

gear something to someone or something to cause something to match something else; to create or adapt something for a specific purpose. □ *Tim geared his speech to his audience.* □ *The newspaper geared its language to a fourth-grade reading level.*

get a dose of one's own medicine to get the same kind of treatment that one gives to other people. □ *Sally is never very friendly. She is going to get a dose of her own medicine someday.* □ *He didn't like getting a dose of his own medicine.*

get a foothold (somewhere) to establish an initial position of support; to reach a starting point. □ *It's difficult to get a foothold in the education market when schools are laying off teachers.* □ *Max's father helped him get a foothold in the textile industry.*

get a handle on something See have a handle on something.

get a kick out of something to be excited or thrilled by something. □ *Mary got a kick out of the funny story.* □ *Didn't you get a kick out of the joke?*

get a load off one's mind to say what one is thinking. □ *He sure talked a long time. I guess he had to get a load off his mind.* □ *You aren't going to like what I'm going to say, but I have to get a load off my mind.*

get a lot of mileage out of something to get a lot of use from something, as if it were a car. □ *Bob always got a lot of mileage* *out of one joke.* □ *I got a lot of mileage out of my TV before it broke down.*

get an eyeful (of someone or something) to see everything; to see a shocking or surprising sight. □ *The office door opened for a minute and I got an eyeful of the interior.* □ *Mary got an eyeful of the company's extravagant spending when she peeked into the conference room.*

get a rise out of someone to get a response, especially an angry response, from someone. □ *I ignored Anne, because she was trying to get a rise out of me.* □ *John's insults got a rise out of David.*

get a word in edgeways See get a word in edgewise.

get a word in edgewise AND **get a word in edgeways** to manage to say something when other people are talking and ignoring one. (Often in the negative. As if one were trying to fit in or squeeze in one's contribution to a conversation.) □ *It was such an exciting conversation that I could hardly get a word in edgewise.* □ *Mary talks so fast that nobody can get a word in edgeways.*

get cold feet to become timid or frightened; to have one's feet seem to freeze with fear. (Also with *have.*) □ *I usually get cold feet when I have to speak in public.* □ *John got cold feet and wouldn't run in the race.* □ *I can't give my speech now. I have cold feet.*

get cracking (on something) to get started on something. □ *I have to get cracking on my homework.* □ *Tom is behind in his share of the work. He has to get cracking.*

get down to brass tacks to begin to talk about important things. □ *Let's get down to brass tacks. We've wasted too much time chatting.* □ *Don't you think that it's about time to get down to brass tacks?*

get down to business AND **get down to work** to begin to get serious; to begin to negotiate or conduct business. □ *All right, everyone. Let's get down to business. There has been enough playing around.* □ *When the president and vice president arrive, we can get down to business.* □ *They're here. Let's get down to work.*

get down to work See get down to business.

get (enough) time to catch one's breath to find enough time to relax or behave normally. (Also with *have.* See also I don't have time to catch my breath. Compare with catch one's breath.)

□ *When things slow down around here, I'll get time to catch my breath.* □ *Sally was so busy she didn't even have enough time to catch her breath.*

get even (with someone) to retaliate against someone; to repay a person for something bad the person has done. □ *I will get even with you for breaking my baseball bat!* □ *Jimmy got even with Bill by punching him in the nose.*

get fresh (with someone) to become overly bold or impertinent. □ *When I tried to kiss Mary, she slapped me and shouted, "Don't get fresh with me!"* □ *I can't stand people who get fresh.*

get married to become united as husband and wife. □ *Bill and Sally got married when they were in college.* □ *We got married in Texas just after we graduated from college.*

get off on a sidetrack to digress; to discuss a topic that is not the main topic. □ *Anne got off on a sidetrack and never returned to her topic.* □ *The ineffective committee got off on one sidetrack after another.*

get off the hook to free oneself from an obligation. □ *They have asked you to lead the parade, and I don't think you can get off the hook.* □ *I couldn't get off the hook no matter how much I pleaded.*

get off to a flying start to have a very successful beginning to something. □ *The new business got off to a flying start with those export orders.* □ *We will need a large donation if the charity is to get off to a flying start.*

get one's feet on the ground AND **have one's feet on the ground** to get firmly established or reestablished. □ *He's new at the job, but soon he'll get his feet on the ground.* □ *Her productivity will improve after she gets her feet on the ground again.*

get one's fingers burned to have a bad experience. □ *I tried that once before and got my fingers burned. I won't try it again.* □ *John got his fingers burned the first time he invested money in the stock market, and now he's afraid to buy stocks again.*

get one's just deserts to get what one deserves. □ *I feel better now that Jane got her just deserts. She really insulted me.* □ *Bill got back exactly the treatment that he gave out. He got his just deserts.*

get one's second wind **1.** [for someone] to achieve stability in breathing again after a period of exhaustion, when one has been continuously exerting oneself. (Also with *have*.) □ *John was having a hard time running until he got his second wind.* □ *Bill had to quit the race because he never got his second wind.* □ *"At last," thought Anne, "I have my second wind. Now I can really swim fast."* **2.** [for someone] to become more active or productive again after a period of slowing down due to exhaustion. (Also with *have*.) □ *I usually get my second wind early in the afternoon.* □ *Mary can work hard again now that she has her second wind.*

get on someone's nerves to irritate someone. □ *Please stop whistling. It's getting on my nerves.* □ *All this arguing is getting on their nerves.*

get out of the wrong side of the bed See get up on the wrong side of the bed.

get rid of someone or something to make oneself free of someone or something. □ *I can't seem to get rid of my younger brother. He follows me everywhere.* □ *Lisa is trying to get rid of the mice in her house.*

get someone's ear to get someone to listen (to one); to have someone's attention. □ *He got my ear and talked for an hour.* □ *While I have your ear, I'd like to tell you about the product that I'm selling.*

get something across (to someone) to succeed in explaining something to someone. □ *The teacher finally got the point across to the students.* □ *Did you ever get it across to her that you want to leave and go home?*

get something into someone's thick head See get something through someone's thick skull.

get something off one's chest to tell something that has been bothering one. (Also with *have*.) □ *I have to get this off my chest. I broke your window with a stone.* □ *I knew I'd feel better when I had that off my chest.*

get something straight to understand something clearly. □ *Let me get this straight. I'm supposed to go there in the morning?* □ *The police officer made sure he had the witness's story straight.*

get something through someone's thick skull AND **get something into someone's thick head** to make someone understand something; to get some information into someone's head.

☐ *He can't seem to get it through his thick skull.* ☐ *If I could get this into my thick head once, I'd remember it.*

get something under way AND **have something under way** to get something started or to have started something. ☐ *The time has come to get this game under way.* ☐ *Now that the president has the meeting under way, I can relax.*

get stars in one's eyes AND **have stars in one's eyes** to be obsessed with movies and the theater. ☐ *Many young people get stars in their eyes at this age.* ☐ *Anne has stars in her eyes. She wants to go to Hollywood.*

get the drift of something to understand the general idea of something. ☐ *I know enough German to get the drift of this article.* ☐ *I don't get the drift of what you're trying to tell me.*

get the feel of something to acquire the ability to do something; to develop the skill or talent for doing something. ☐ *Don't worry. You'll get the feel of it.* ☐ *I finally got the feel of dancing to fast music.*

get the final word See get the last word.

get the last laugh to laugh at or ridicule someone who has laughed at or ridiculed one; to put someone in the same bad position that one was once in oneself. (Also with *have.*) ☐ *John laughed when I got a D on the final exam. I got the last laugh, though. He failed the course.* ☐ *Mr. Smith said I was foolish when I bought an old building. I had the last laugh when I sold it a month later for twice what I paid for it.*

get the last word AND **get the final word** to make the final point (in an argument); to make the final decision (in some matter). (Also with *have.*) ☐ *The boss gets the last word in hiring.* ☐ *Why do you always have to have the final word in an argument?*

get the runaround to receive a series of excuses, delays, and referrals. ☐ *You'll get the runaround if you ask to see the manager.* ☐ *I hate it when I get the runaround.* ALSO: **give someone the runaround** to give someone a series of excuses, delays, and referrals. ☐ *If you ask to see the manager, they'll give you the runaround.*

get the shock of one's life to receive a serious (emotional) shock. (Also with *have*.) □ *I opened the telegram and got the shock of my life.* □ *I had the shock of my life when I won $5,000.*

get the upper hand (on someone) to get into a position superior to someone; to get the advantage over someone. (Also with *have*.) □ *John is always trying to get the upper hand on me.* □ *He never ends up having the upper hand, though.*

getting on (in years) getting old; old. □ *Mom is getting on. She can't travel as much as she used to.* □ *Mrs. Hathaway is getting on in years, but she is still perfectly able to take care of herself.*

get to one's feet to stand up. □ *On a signal from the director, the singers got to their feet.* □ *I was so weak, I could hardly get to my feet.*

get to someone to affect someone emotionally in a bad way; to bother someone. □ *Working with abandoned children eventually got to David, and he had to transfer to another department.* □ *Nothing gets to me like seeing people litter.*

get to the point See come to the point.

get up enough nerve (to do something) to get brave enough to do something. □ *I could never get up enough nerve to sing in public.* □ *I'd do it if I could get up enough nerve, but I'm shy.*

get up on the wrong side of the bed AND **get out of the wrong side of the bed** to get up in the morning in a bad mood. (As if the choice of the side of the bed makes a difference in one's humor.) □ *What's wrong with you? Did you get up on the wrong side of the bed today?* □ *Excuse me for being grouchy. I got out of the wrong side of the bed.*

get wind of something AND **catch wind of something** to learn of something; to hear about something. □ *The police got wind of the illegal drug deal.* □ *John caught wind of the gossip being spread about him.*

Get your nose out of my business. See Mind your own business.

give-and-take the cooperation between two sides who are bargaining for something; the essence of negotiation. □ *The union asked for a little give-and-take from management.* □ *The mediator praised the give-and-take shown by both sides.*

give birth to someone or **some creature** to bring a baby or other offspring into the world through birth. □ *Mary gave birth to a lovely baby girl.* □ *The raccoon gave birth to six little raccoons.*

give birth to something to create, start, or yield something. □ *Poverty and a lack of opportunity give birth to crime and more poverty.* □ *The discovery of gold in the West gave birth to the settlement of California.*

Give me a chance! Please be patient! □ *I'm doing the best I can. Please give me a chance!* □ *Give me a chance! I can't do everything at once.*

Give me five! AND **Give me (some) skin!; Skin me!; Slip me five!; Slip me some skin!** Shake my hand!; Slap my hand in greeting! (Slang.) □ *"Yo, Tom! Give me five!" shouted Henry, raising his hand.* □ *BOB: Hey, man! Skin me! BILL: How you doing, Bob?*

Give me (some) skin! See Give me five!

a **given** a fact that is taken for granted; a fact that is assumed. □ *That Mary will go to college is a given. The question is what she is going to study.* □ *It is a given that the earth revolves around the sun.*

given to doing something likely to do something; inclined to do something habitually. □ *Mary is given to singing in the shower.* □ *Bob is given to shouting when things don't go his way.*

give one a new lease on life to give someone a renewed and revitalized outlook on life. □ *Getting the job offer gave me a new lease on life.* □ *When I got out of the hospital, I felt as if I had gotten a new lease on life.*

give (one's) notice to quit one's job. □ *Did you hear that James is leaving? He gave his notice yesterday.* □ *Lisa gave notice today. She got a job offer from another company.*

give someone a blank check to give someone permission to spend an unlimited amount of money. □ *Tom gave the mechanic a blank check to make the repairs.* □ *The foundation gave the agency a blank check to plan a program.*

give someone a buzz See give someone a ring.

give someone a hand 1. AND **lend someone a hand** to help someone. □ *Can you give me a hand carrying this box, please?*

□ *After the hurricane, everyone lent a hand to help clean up the town.* **2.** to applaud someone. □ *The audience gave the singer a big hand.* □ *The crowd rose and gave the politician a hand.*

give someone a pat on the back to praise someone with words. □ *My boss gave me a pat on the back over the telephone.* □ *When I see Tom, I will give him a pat on the back for his patience.*

give someone a piece of one's mind to bawl someone out; to tell someone off. □ *I've had enough from John. I'm going to give him a piece of my mind.* □ *Sally, stop it, or I'll give you a piece of my mind.*

give someone a ring AND **give someone a buzz** to call someone on the telephone. (*Ring* and *buzz* refer to the bell in a telephone.) □ *Nice talking to you. Give me a ring sometime.* □ *Give me a buzz when you're in town.*

give someone hell to scold someone severely. □ *David gave his son hell for telling lies.* □ *Don't give me hell about that! I didn't do it!*

give someone or something a wide berth to keep a reasonable distance from someone or something; to steer clear of someone or something. (Originally referred to sailing ships.) □ *The dog we are approaching is very mean. Better give it a wide berth.* □ *Give Mary a wide berth. She's in a very bad mood.*

give someone the runaround See under get the runaround.

give something a lick and a promise to do something poorly— quickly and carelessly. □ *John! You didn't clean your room! You just gave it a lick and a promise.* □ *This time, Tom, comb your hair. It looks as if you just gave it a lick and a promise.*

give something a shot AND **take a shot at something** to try something. □ *I have never dived before, but I will give it a shot.* □ *Tom decided to take a shot at writing a poem.*

give something a whirl to make a try at something. □ *If at first you don't succeed, give it another whirl.* □ *John gave bowling a whirl last night.*

Give you a lift? See Could I give you a lift?

gnash one's teeth to slash about with the teeth. □ *Bill clenched his fists and gnashed his teeth in anger.* □ *The wolf gnashed its teeth and chased after the deer.*

(Go ahead,) make my day! 1. Just try to do me harm or disobey me. I will enjoy punishing you. (From a phrase said in a movie where the person saying the phrase is holding a gun on a villain and would really like the villain to do something that would justify firing the gun. Now a cliché.) □ *The crook reached into his jacket for his wallet. The cop, thinking the crook was about to draw a gun, said, "Go ahead, make my day!"* □ *As Bill pulled back his clenched fist to strike Tom, who is much bigger and stronger than Bill, Tom said, "Make my day!"* **2.** Go ahead, ruin my day!; Go ahead, give me the bad news. (A sarcastic version of sense 1.) □ *TOM (standing in the doorway): Hello, I'm with the Internal Revenue Service. Could I come in? MARY: Go ahead, make my day!* □ *SALLY: I've got some bad news for you. JOHN: Go ahead, make my day!*

go away empty-handed to leave without what one came for. (Compare with come away empty-handed.) □ *I hate for you to go away empty-handed, but I cannot afford to contribute any money.* □ *They came hoping for some food, but they had to go away empty-handed.*

go crazy to become crazy, disoriented, or frustrated. □ *It is so busy here that I think I will go crazy.* □ *Bob went crazy because his car got a flat tire.*

go downhill to become worse; to worsen. □ *Everything went downhill for the team when the star athlete retired.* □ *Employee morale went downhill after the layoffs.*

go down in history to be remembered as historically important. (A cliché.) □ *Bill is so great. I'm sure that he'll go down in history.* □ *This is the greatest party of the century. I bet it'll go down in history.*

Go fly a kite! Go away and stop bothering me. □ *You are a real bother. Go fly a kite!* □ *You are taking too much of my time. Go fly a kite!*

go haywire to begin to function incorrectly. □ *The telephone went haywire during the storm.* □ *My radio goes haywire whenever a plane flies overhead.*

the **going** the condition of a path of travel or progress. (Compare with slow going.) □ *The going was rough through the mountains.* □ *I decided to sell my stock while the going was still good.*

the **going rate** the current rate. □ *The going interest rate for your account is 5%.* □ *Our babysitter charges us the going rate.*

go in one ear and out the other [for something] to be heard and then forgotten. (Not literal.) □ *Everything I say to you seems to go in one ear and out the other. Why don't you pay attention?* □ *I can't concentrate. Things people say to me just go in one ear and out the other.*

go into detail to give all the details; to present and discuss the details. □ *The clerk went into detail about the product with the customer.* □ *I just want a simple answer. Don't go into detail.*

go into hiding to conceal oneself in a hidden place for a period of time. □ *The political dissident went into hiding.* □ *After robbing the bank, the bandits went into hiding for months.*

go into hock to go into debt. □ *We will have to go into hock to buy a house.* □ *I go further into hock every time I use my credit card.*

go into one's song and dance about something to start giving one's usual or typical explanations and excuses about something. (A cliché. *One's* can be replaced with *the same old.* Does not involve singing or dancing.) □ *Please don't go into your song and dance about how you always tried to do what was right.* □ *John went into his song and dance about how he won the war all by himself.* □ *He always goes into the same old song and dance every time he makes a mistake.*

Go jump in the lake! Go away!; Stop bothering me! □ *Stop pestering me! Go jump in the lake!* □ *If you think you can push me around like that, you can just go jump in the lake.*

go on to happen; to occur. □ *What is going on here?* □ *Something is going on in the center of town. Can you hear the sirens?*

go on a fishing expedition to attempt to discover information. (Also used literally. As if one were sending bait into the invisible depths of a body of water, trying to catch something, but nothing in particular.) □ *We are going to have to go on a fishing expedition to try to find the facts.* □ *One lawyer went on a fishing expedition in court, and the other lawyer objected.*

go on a rampage to behave or react wildly or violently. □ *The angry bull went on a rampage and broke the fence.* □ *My boss went on a rampage because the report wasn't finished.*

goose bumps AND **goose pimples** prickly bumps on the skin due to fear or excitement. □ *When he sings, I get goose bumps.* □ *I never get goose pimples.* □ *That really scared her. Now she's got goose pimples.*

goose pimples See goose bumps.

go (out) on strike [for a group of people] to quit working at their jobs until certain demands are met. □ *If we don't have a contract by noon tomorrow, we'll go out on strike.* □ *The entire work force went on strike at noon today.*

go out with someone to go on a date with someone; to spend an evening with someone doing something such as seeing a movie or eating a meal. □ *John would like to go out with Mary, but is too shy to ask her.* □ *Would you go out with me sometime?*

go overboard 1. to fall off or out of a boat or ship. □ *My fishing pole just went overboard. I'm afraid it's lost.* □ *That man just went overboard. I think he jumped.* **2.** to do too much; to be extravagant. □ *Look, Sally, let's have a nice party, but don't go overboard. It doesn't need to be fancy.* □ *Okay, you can buy a big comfortable car, but don't go overboard.*

go over someone's head 1. [for the intellectual content of something] to be too difficult for someone to understand. (As if it flew over one's head rather than entering into one's store of knowledge.) □ *All that talk about computers went over my head.* □ *I hope my lecture didn't go over the students' heads.* **2.** to carry a request to someone's boss, supervisor, or superior. □ *I am angry because you went over my head rather than discussing the problem with me.* □ *If you don't agree with my proposal, I will go over your head and get your boss to agree!*

go over something with a fine-tooth comb AND **search something with a fine-tooth comb** to search through something very carefully. (As if one were searching for something very tiny lost in some kind of fiber.) □ *I can't find my passport. I went over the whole house with a fine-tooth comb.* □ *I searched this place with a fine-tooth comb and didn't find my ring.*

the **gospel truth** the undeniable, absolute truth. □ *The witness swore he was telling the gospel truth.* □ *I told my parents the gospel truth about how the vase broke.*

go straight to stop breaking the law and lead a lawful life instead. □ *The judge encouraged the thief to go straight.* □ *After Bob was arrested, he promised his mother he would go straight.*

go the distance to do the whole amount; to play the entire game; to run the whole race. (Originally used in sports.) □ *That horse runs fast. I hope it can go the distance.* □ *This is going to be a long, hard project. I hope I can go the distance.*

go through channels to proceed by consulting the proper persons or offices. (*Channels* refers to the route a piece of business must take through a hierarchy or a bureaucracy.) □ *If you want an answer to your questions, you'll have to go through channels.* □ *If you know the answers, why do I have to go through channels?*

go to bed to go to where one's bed is, get into it, and go to sleep. □ *It's time for me to go to bed.* □ *I want to go to bed, but there is too much work to do.*

go to Davy Jones's locker to go to the bottom of the sea. (Thought of as a nautical expression.) □ *My camera fell overboard and went to Davy Jones's locker.* □ *My uncle was a sailor. He went to Davy Jones's locker during a terrible storm.*

go to pot AND **go to the dogs** to go to ruin; to deteriorate. □ *My whole life seems to be going to pot.* □ *My lawn is going to pot. I had better weed it.* □ *The government is going to the dogs.*

go to the bathroom to urinate; to defecate. □ *Jimmy has to go to the bathroom right now.* □ *Mommy, the puppy is going to the bathroom on the carpet.*

go to the dogs See go to pot.

go to the lavatory See go to the toilet.

go to the toilet AND **go to the lavatory** to use a toilet for defecation or urination. □ *Jimmy washed his hands after he went to the toilet.* □ *Excuse me, I have to go to the lavatory.*

go to the wall to fail or be defeated after being pushed to the extreme. □ *We really went to the wall on that deal.* □ *The company went to the wall because of that contract. Now it's bankrupt.*

go to town to work hard or fast. (Also used literally.) □ *Look at all those ants working. They are really going to town.* □ *Come on, you guys! Let's go to town. We have to finish this job before noon.*

go without AND **do without** to manage while not having any; to not have any of something. □ *We were a poor family and usually went without.* □ *I didn't have enough money to buy a new coat so I did without.*

grab a bite (to eat) to get something to eat; to get food that can be eaten quickly. □ *I need a few minutes to grab a bite to eat.* □ *Bob often tries to grab a bite between meetings.*

graced with something made elegant by means of some ornament or decoration. □ *The altar was graced with lovely white flowers.* □ *The end of the beautiful day was graced with a lovely sunset.*

grace someone or something with one's presence to honor someone or something with one's presence. □ *"How nice of you to grace us with your presence," Mr. Wilson told Mary sarcastically as she entered the classroom late.* □ *The banquet was graced with the presence of the governor.*

grain of truth the smallest amount of truth. □ *The attorney was unable to find a grain of truth in the defendant's testimony.* □ *If there were a grain of truth to your statement, I would trust you.*

grate on someone('s nerves) to annoy someone; to bother someone. □ *My obnoxious brother is grating on my nerves.* □ *Your whining really grates on me.*

a **great deal** much; a lot. □ *You can learn a great deal about nature by watching television.* □ *This is a serious problem and it worries me a great deal.*

grind to a halt to slow to a stop; to run down. □ *By the end of the day, the factory had ground to a halt.* □ *The car ground to a halt, and we got out to stretch our legs.*

grip someone's attention to attract and hold someone's attention. □ *The scary movie gripped my attention.* □ *The professor's interesting lecture gripped the attention of all the students.*

grit one's teeth to grind one's teeth together in anger or determination. □ *I was so mad, all I could do was stand there and grit my teeth.* □ *All through the race, Sally was gritting her teeth. She was really determined.*

groan under the weight of something to suffer under the burden or domination of someone or something. □ *John groaned* *under the weight of his new responsibilities.* □ *The servant groaned under the weight of his job.*

grounded in fact based on facts. □ *This movie is grounded in fact.* □ *The stories in this book are all grounded in actual fact.*

grounds for something a basis or cause for legal action such as a lawsuit. □ *Your negligence is grounds for a lawsuit.* □ *Is infidelity grounds for divorce in this state?*

grow to do something to gradually begin to do something. (Used especially with verbs such as *feel, know, like, need, respect, sense, suspect, think, want,* and *wonder.*) □ *I grew to hate Bob over a period of years.* □ *As I grew to know Bob, I began to like him.*

grunt work work that is hard and thankless. □ *During the summer, I earned money doing grunt work.* □ *I did all the grunt work on the project, but my boss got all the credit.*

guest of honor a guest who gets special attention from everyone; the person for whom a party, celebration, or ceremony is given. □ *Bob is the guest of honor, and many people will make speeches about him.* □ *The guests of honor sat at the front of the room on a small platform.*

gulp for air to eagerly or desperately try to get air or a breath. □ *Tom gulped for air after trying to hold his breath for three minutes.* □ *Mary came up out of the water, gulping for air.*

gut feeling AND **gut reaction; gut response** a personal, intuitive feeling or response. □ *I have a gut feeling that something bad is going to happen.* □ *My gut reaction is that we should hire Susan for the job.*

gut reaction See gut feeling.

gut response See gut feeling.

gyp someone out of something to deceive someone in order to get something of value. □ *The salesclerk gypped me out of a dollar.* □ *The taxi driver tried to gyp me out of a fortune by driving all over town.*

hale and hearty well and healthy. □ *Doesn't Anne look hale and hearty?* □ *I don't feel hale and hearty. I'm really tired.*

halfhearted (about someone or something) unenthusiastic about someone or something. □ *Anne was halfhearted about the choice of Sally for president.* □ *She didn't look halfhearted to me. She looked angry.*

Hang it all! Oh, what a bother!; How annoying! □ *Hang it all! I can't seem to add up these figures correctly.* □ *I'm going to be late. Hang it all!*

Hang on! Be prepared for fast or rough movement. □ *Hang on! Here we go!* □ *The airplane passengers suddenly seemed weightless. Someone shouted, "Hang on!"*

hardly have time to breathe to be very busy. (See also **I don't have time to catch my breath.**) □ *This was such a busy day. I hardly had time to breathe.* □ *They made him work so hard that he hardly had time to breathe.*

hard of hearing [of someone] unable to hear well or partially deaf. □ *Please speak loudly. I am hard of hearing.* □ *Tom is hard of hearing, but is not totally deaf.*

has seen better days is in bad condition. □ *My old car has seen better days, but at least it's still running.* □ *She's seen better days, it's true, but she's still lots of fun.*

hate someone's guts to hate someone very much. (Informal and rude.) □ *Oh, Bob is terrible. I hate his guts!* □ *You may hate my guts for saying so, but I think you're getting gray hair.*

have a ball to have a good time; to have fun. □ *We had a ball on our vacation.* □ *The kids had a ball playing in the leaves.*

have a bee in one's bonnet to have an idea or a thought remain in one's mind; to have an obsession. (The bee is a thought that is inside one's head, which is inside a bonnet.) □ *I have a bee in my bonnet that you'd be a good manager.* □ *I had a bee in my bonnet about swimming. I couldn't stop wanting to go swimming.* ALSO: **put a bee in someone's bonnet** to give someone an idea (about something). □ *Somebody put a bee in my bonnet that we should go to a movie.* □ *Who put a bee in your bonnet?*

have a bone to pick (with someone) to have a matter to discuss with someone; to have something to argue about with someone. □ *Hey, Bill. I have a bone to pick with you. Where is the money you owe me?* □ *I had a bone to pick with her, but she was so sweet that I forgot about it.* □ *You always have a bone to pick.*

have a brush with something to have a brief contact with something; to have an experience with something. (Especially with the law. Sometimes *a close brush.*) □ *Anne had a close brush with the law. She was nearly arrested for speeding.* □ *When I was younger, I had a brush with scarlet fever, but I got over it.*

have a familiar ring [for a story or an explanation] to sound familiar. □ *Your excuse has a familiar ring. Have you done this before?* □ *This term paper has a familiar ring. I think it has been copied.*

have a frog in one's throat to have a feeling of hoarseness. □ *I cannot speak more clearly. I have a frog in my throat.* □ *I had a frog in my throat, and the telephone receptionist couldn't understand me.*

have a go at something to make an attempt at (doing) something. □ *At the carnival, my friend urged me to have a go at one of the games.* □ *If you can't open the pickle jar, let me have a go at it.*

have a good command of something to possess the understanding necessary to do something well. □ *Anne has a good command of the German language.* □ *Dave has a good command of his computer's operations.*

have a good eye for something See have an eye for something.

have a good head on one's shoulders to have common sense; to be sensible and intelligent. □ *Mary doesn't do well in school, but she has a good head on her shoulders.* □ *John has a good head on his shoulders and can be depended on to give good advice.*

have a hand in something to have an influence on something. □ *Tom's grandparents have always had a hand in helping him.* □ *Who had the biggest hand in your education?*

have a handle on something AND **get a handle on something** to have or get control of something; to have or get an understanding of something. □ *Get a handle on your temper and calm down.* □ *The police chief had a handle on the potential riot situation.*

have a head for something have the mental capacity for something. □ *Jane has a good head for directions and never gets lost.* □ *Bill doesn't have a head for figures and should never become an accountant.*

have a heart to be compassionate; to be generous and forgiving; to have an especially compassionate heart. □ *Oh, have a heart! Give me some help!* □ *If Anne had a heart, she'd have made us feel more welcome.*

have a heart of gold to be generous, kind, sincere, and friendly. (Not literal.) □ *Mary is such a lovely person. She has a heart of gold.* □ *You think Tom stole your watch? Impossible! He has a heart of gold.*

have a hold on someone to have a strong and secure influence on someone. □ *The strange religious cult seemed to have a strong hold on its followers.* □ *The drug has a hold on the minds of those who use it.*

have a look at someone or something See take a look at someone or something.

have a look for someone or something See take a look for someone or something.

have an ear for something to have the ability to learn music or languages. □ *Bill doesn't have an ear for music. He can't carry a tune.* □ *Mary has a good ear for languages.*

have an eye for something AND **have a good eye for something** the ability to see small details; the ability to see the difference between two things that are similar. □ *The designer had a good eye for color.* □ *The teacher has an eye for identifying promising students.*

have an eye out (for someone or something) AND **keep an eye out (for someone or something)** to watch for the arrival or appearance of someone or something. (The *an* can be replaced with *one's.*) □ *Please try to have an eye out for the bus.* □ *Keep an eye out for rain.* □ *Have your eye out for a raincoat on sale.* □ *Okay. I'll keep my eye out.*

have an in (with someone) to have a way to request a special favor from someone; to have influence with someone. (The *in* is a noun.) □ *Do you have an in with the mayor? I have to ask him a favor.* □ *Sorry, I don't have an in, but I know someone who does.*

have an itch for something to have a desire for something. □ *I have an itch for a nice cool glass of lemonade.* □ *Who besides me has an itch for pizza?*

have an itch to do something to have a desire to do something. □ *I have an itch to see a movie tonight.* □ *Tom has an itch to go swimming.*

have a nose for something to have the talent for finding something. □ *Police dogs have a good nose for drugs.* □ *The reporter has a nose for news.*

have a one-track mind to think entirely or almost entirely about one subject. □ *Adolescent boys often have one-track minds. All they're interested in is the opposite sex.* □ *Bob has a one-track mind. He can only talk about football.*

have a passion for someone or something to have a strong feeling of need or desire for someone, something, or some activity. □ *Mary has a great passion for chocolate.* □ *John has a passion for fishing, so he fishes as often as he can.*

have a peep AND **take a peep** to look quickly, sometimes through a small hole. □ *Have a peep into the refrigerator and see if we need any milk.* □ *I took a peep at the comet through the telescope.*

have a penchant for something to have a liking for something; to have an inclination toward doing something. □ *My roommate has a penchant for cooking elaborate dinners.* □ *My nosy neighbor has a penchant for gossip.*

have a poor command of something to lack sufficient knowledge about a task or process. □ *I have a poor command of typing.* □ *If I had such a poor command of algebra, I'd study more.*

have arrived to have reached a position of power, authority, or prominence. □ *Jane saw her picture on the cover of the magazine and felt that she had finally arrived.* □ *When I got an office with a window, I knew that I had arrived.*

have a run-in with someone to have an unpleasant and troublesome encounter with someone. □ *I had a run-in with Anne at the party, so I left early.* □ *David had a small run-in with the law last night.*

have a stab at something AND **take a stab at something** to try something; to make a try at doing something. □ *I would like to have a stab at operating the bulldozer.* □ *Why don't you take a stab at painting the fence?*

have a sweet tooth to desire many sweet foods—especially candy and pastries. (As if a certain tooth had a craving for sweets.) □ *I have a sweet tooth, and if I'm not careful, I'll really get fat.* □ *John eats candy all the time. He must have a sweet tooth.*

have a taste for something to desire a particular food, drink, or experience. □ *The Smiths have a taste for adventure and take exotic vacations.* □ *When she was pregnant, Mary often had a taste for pickles.*

Have at it. Start doing it.; Start eating it. □ *JOHN: Here's your hamburger. Have at it. JANE: Thanks. Where's the mustard?* □ *JOHN: Did you notice? The driveway needs sweeping. JANE: Here's the broom. Have at it.*

have a vested interest in something to have a personal or biased interest, often financial, in something. □ *Margaret has a vested interest in wanting her father to sell the family firm. She has shares in it and would make a large profit.* □ *Bob has a vested interest in keeping the village traffic-free. He has a summer home there.*

have a weight problem to be fat; to be heavy. □ *He had a weight problem when he was a teenager, but he slimmed down once he started exercising.* □ *She has a weight problem, but she's a lovely woman.*

have a word with someone to have a short chat with someone, usually a private chat. □ *Jane's boss asked if he could have a word with her.* □ *I had a word with Max about his work performance.*

have bats in one's belfry to be slightly crazy. (The belfry—a bell tower—represents one's head or brains. The bats represent an infestation of confusion.) □ *Poor old Tom has bats in his belfry.* □ *Don't act so silly, John. People will think you have bats in your belfry.*

have bigger fish to fry AND **have other fish to fry** to have other things to do; to have more important things to do. □ *I can't take time for your problem. I have other fish to fry.* □ *I won't waste time on your question. I have bigger fish to fry.*

have clean hands to be guiltless. (As if the guilty person would have bloody or dirty hands.) □ *Don't look at me. I have clean hands.* □ *The police took him in, but let him go again because he had clean hands.*

have contact with someone to have a link to someone that results in communication; to be in communication with someone. □ *I have had no contact with Bill since he left town.* □ *Tom had contact with a known criminal last month.*

have dibs on something to reserve something for oneself; to claim something for oneself. □ *I have dibs on the last piece of cake.* □ *John has dibs on the last piece again. It isn't fair.*

have egg on one's face to be embarrassed because of an error that is obvious to everyone. (Rarely literal.) □ *Bob has egg on his face because he wore jeans to the party and everyone else wore formal clothing.* □ *John was completely wrong about the weather for the picnic. It snowed! Now he has egg on his face.*

have feet of clay [for a strong person] to have a defect of character. □ *All human beings have feet of clay. No one is perfect.* □ *Sally was popular and successful. She was nearly fifty before she learned that she, too, had feet of clay.*

have got a lot of nerve AND **have got some nerve** to have a lot of gall and impudence. □ *You've got a lot of nerve to phone me so late at night!* □ *You've got some nerve to treat me so rudely!*

have got some nerve See have got a lot of nerve.

have money to burn to have lots of money; to have more money than one needs; to have so much money that some can be wasted. □ *Look at the way Tom buys things. You'd think he had money to burn.* □ *If I had money to burn, I'd just put it in the bank.*

have nothing to do with someone or something AND **[not] have anything to do with someone or something 1.** to have no interaction with someone or something; to refrain from dealing with someone or something; to not concern oneself with someone or something. □ *I don't like Mike, and I won't have anything to do with the books he writes.* □ *Bob has had nothing to do with Mary since she quit her job. I think he's mad at her.* **2.** to be entirely unrelated to someone or something; to be not connected or associated with someone or something in any way. (Compare with **have something to do with someone or something.**) □ *We were not gossiping about you. In fact, our conversation did not have anything to do with you.* □ *Your point has nothing to do with my argument. It's totally irrelevant.* □ *I didn't start the fire. I had nothing to do with it!*

have one's back to the wall to be in a defensive position. □ *He'll have to give in. He has his back to the wall.* □ *How can I bargain when I have my back to the wall?*

have one's feet on the ground See get one's feet on the ground.

have one's finger in the pie to be involved in something. (Not literal.) □ *I like to have my finger in the pie so I can make sure things go my way.* □ *As long as John has his finger in the pie, things will happen slowly.*

have one's finger in the till AND **have one's hand in the till** to steal money from one's employer. □ *James couldn't afford that car on just his salary. He must have his hand in the till.* □ *Sally was outraged when she found that one of her salesclerks had his finger in the till.*

have one's hand in the till See have one's finger in the till.

have one's heart in one's mouth to feel strongly emotional about someone or something. □ *"Gosh, Mary," said John, "I have my heart in my mouth whenever I see you."* □ *My father has his heart in his mouth whenever he hears the national anthem.* ALSO: **one's heart is in one's mouth** one feels strongly emotional. □ *It was a touching scene. My heart was in my mouth the whole time.*

have one's heart set on something to desire and expect something. □ *Jane has her heart set on going to London.* □ *Bob will be disappointed. He had his heart set on going to college this year.*

have one's nose in a book to be reading a book; to read books all the time. □ *Bob has his nose in a book every time I see him.* □ *He always has his nose in a book. He never gets any exercise.*

have one's sights trained on something See train one's sights on something.

have other fish to fry See have bigger fish to fry.

have second thoughts about someone or something to have doubts about someone or something. □ *I'm beginning to have second thoughts about Tom.* □ *We now have second thoughts about going to Canada.*

have [some] bearing on something [for something] to affect or influence something else. (Usually with *any, some, little,* or *no.*) □ *The worker's opinion has no bearing on the boss's decision.* □ *What bearing does John's decision have on the situation?* □ *This piece of evidence has little bearing on the legal case.*

have someone dead to rights to catch someone in a situation that clearly demonstrates the person's guilt. □ *The police burst in on the robbers while they were at work. They had the robbers dead to rights.* □ *All right, Tom! I have you dead to rights! Get your hands out of the cookie jar.*

have someone in one's pocket to have control over someone. □ *Don't worry about the mayor. She'll cooperate. I have her in my pocket.* □ *John will do just what I tell him. I have him and his brother in my pocket.*

have someone over to invite someone as a guest to one's house. □ *When can we have Aunt Jane over for dinner?* □ *I would love to have you over some time.*

have someone pegged as something See peg someone as something.

have someone's blood on one's hands to be responsible for someone's death; to be guilty of causing someone's death. □ *The murderer had the teenager's blood on his hands.* □ *If people die because your product is dangerous, you will have their blood on your hands!*

have something down pat to have learned or memorized something perfectly. □ *I have practiced my speech until I have it down* *pat.* □ *Tom has his part in the play down pat. He won't make any mistakes.*

have something hanging over one's head to have something bothering or worrying one; to have a deadline worrying one. □ *I keep worrying about getting fired. I hate to have something like that hanging over my head.* □ *I have a history paper that is hanging over my head. It's due on Monday.*

have something to do with someone or something to be associated with or related to someone or something. (The first *something* does not vary. For the negative form, see **have nothing to do with someone or something**.) □ *Does your dislike for Sally have something to do with the way she insulted you?* □ *My illness has something to do with my lungs.*

have something under way See **get something under way.**

have stars in one's eyes See **get stars in one's eyes.**

have the gall to do something to have sufficient arrogance to do something. □ *I bet you don't have the gall to argue with the mayor.* □ *Only Jane has the gall to ask the boss for a second raise this month.*

have the makings of something to possess the qualities that are needed for something. □ *The young boy had the makings of a fine baseball player.* □ *My boss has all the makings of a prison warden.*

have the shoe on the other foot to experience the opposite situation (from a previous situation). (Also used with *is* instead of *have.* See the examples.) □ *I used to be a student, and now I'm the teacher. Now I have the shoe on the other foot.* □ *You were mean to me when you thought I was cheating. Now that I have caught you cheating, the shoe is on the other foot.*

have to do with something to be associated with or related to something. □ *Sally's unhappiness has to do with the way you insulted her.* □ *My illness has to do with my stomach.*

have too many irons in the fire to be doing too many things at once. (A cliché. As if a blacksmith had more things get hot in the fire than could possibly be dealt with.) □ *Tom had too many irons in the fire and missed some important deadlines.* □ *It's better if you don't have too many irons in the fire.*

have two strikes against one to have several things against one; to be in a position where success is unlikely. □ *Poor Bob had two strikes against him when he tried to explain where he was last night.* □ *I can't win. I have two strikes against me before I start.*

have words to argue. □ *From the sound of things, Bill and his father had words last night.* □ *We had words on the subject of money.*

hazard a guess to make a guess. □ *Even if you don't know, please hazard a guess.* □ *If you don't know the size, hazard a guess.*

hazard an opinion to give an opinion. □ *Anne asked the attorney to hazard an opinion about the strength of her lawsuit.* □ *Don't feel like you have to hazard an opinion on something you know nothing about.*

a **head** AND **per head** for each person; for each individual. □ *How much do you charge per head for dinner?* □ *It costs eight dollars a head.*

hearing impaired deaf or nearly deaf. □ *This program is closed-captioned for the hearing impaired.* □ *His mother happens to be hearing impaired, so he learned to sign at an early age.*

a **heartbeat away from something** to be next in line for a position; to be very close to achieving something. (As if one will attain the position at the moment that the heart of the person who currently occupies it stops beating. Especially in reference to U.S. presidential succession.) □ *The vice president is just a heartbeat away from being president.* □ *The prince was only a heartbeat away from being king.*

help oneself (to something) to take something for oneself without asking permission. □ *The thief helped himself to the money in the safe.* □ *Help yourself to more dessert.*

Here we go again. The same thing is happening again.; This is the same problem all over again.; This is yet another repetition of what just happened or what was just said. □ *Here we go again, the same problem for the third time.* □ *Here we go again. John is going to tell his favorite joke. He's already told it twice today.*

Here you are. 1. So, this is where you have been.; Now I have found you. (The stress is on *here*.) □ *Here you are. I wondered where you were.* □ *Oh, here you are. Where have you been?* **2.** This is where you want to be.; I have brought you to where you wanted to go. □ *"Here you are," said the taxi driver. This is your house.* □ *Here you are, right at your bus stop.* **3.** This is yours.; This is the meal your ordered.; This is what you requested. □ *Here you are. The plate is very hot.* □ *Here you are, a salad with a nice creamy dressing.*

hinge on something to depend on something. □ *Everything hinges on Anne's timely arrival at the party.* □ *My acceptance of the promotion hinges on whether or not I also get a raise in pay.*

hit a plateau to reach a higher level of activity, sales, production, output, etc., and then stop and remain unchanged. □ *When my sales hit a plateau, my boss gave me a pep talk.* □ *When production hit a plateau, the company built a new factory.*

hitch a ride to get a ride from a passing motorist; to make a sign with one's thumb that indicates to passing drivers that one is begging for a ride. □ *My car broke down on the highway, and I had to hitch a ride to get back to town.* □ *Sometimes it's dangerous to hitch a ride with a stranger.*

hit home AND **strike home** to really make sense; [for a comment] to make a very good point. □ *Mary's criticism of my clothes hit home, so I changed.* □ *The teacher's comment struck home and the student vowed to work harder.*

hit it off (with someone) to become friends with someone fairly fast; to get along well with someone one has just met. □ *Bill seems to hit it off with Bob.* □ *Mary and Jane hit it off quite nicely.*

hit someone hard to affect someone's emotions strongly. □ *The death of his friend hit John hard.* □ *The investor was hit hard by the falling stock prices.*

hit (someone) like a ton of bricks to surprise, startle, or shock someone. □ *Suddenly, the truth hit me like a ton of bricks.* □ *The sudden tax increase hit like a ton of bricks. Everyone became angry.*

hit someone (right) between the eyes to become completely apparent; to surprise or impress someone. □ *Suddenly, it hit me right between the eyes. John and Mary were in love.* □ *Then—as he was talking—the exact nature of the evil plan hit me between the eyes.*

hit the bull's-eye 1. to hit the center area of a circular target. (Literal.) □ *The archer hit the bull's-eye three times in a row.* □ *I didn't* *hit the bull's-eye even once.* **2.** to achieve a goal perfectly. □ *Your idea really hit the bull's-eye. Thank you!* □ *Jill has a lot of insight. She knows how to hit the bull's-eye.*

hit the nail (right) on the head to do exactly the right thing; to do something in the most effective and efficient way. (A cliché.) □ *You've spotted the flaw, Sally. You hit the nail on the head.* □ *Bob doesn't say much, but every now and then he hits the nail right on the head.*

hit the sack to go to bed. □ *It's late. It's time to hit the sack.* □ *What time did you hit the sack last night?*

a **hive of activity** a location where things are very busy. □ *The hotel lobby was a hive of activity each morning.* □ *During the holidays, the shopping center is a hive of activity.*

hold a grudge (against someone) to continue to feel resentment against someone. □ *John won't talk to me because he's holding a grudge against me.* □ *I held a grudge against my sister for 25 years.*

hold one's end (of the bargain) up AND **hold up one's end (of the bargain)** to do one's part as agreed; to attend to one's responsibilities as agreed. □ *Tom has to learn to cooperate. He must hold up his end of the bargain.* □ *If you don't hold your end up, the whole project will fail.*

hold one's peace to remain silent. □ *Bill was unable to hold his peace any longer. "Don't do it!" he cried.* □ *Quiet, John. Hold your peace for a little while longer.*

hold one's tongue to refrain from speaking; to refrain from saying something unpleasant. (Not literal.) □ *I felt like scolding her, but I held my tongue.* □ *Hold your tongue, John. You can't talk to me that way.*

hold someone hostage to keep someone as a hostage. □ *The terrorists planned to hold everyone hostage in the airplane.* □ *My neighbor was held hostage in his own home by a robber.*

hold someone or something in high regard to have very great respect for someone or something; to admire someone or something greatly. □ *We hold our employees in very high regard.* □ *I do not hold Bob's abilities in high regard.*

hold someone's attention to keep someone's attention; to keep someone interested. □ *The boring teacher could not hold the* *students' attention.* □ *The mystery novel held my attention and I couldn't put it down.*

hold the fort to take care of a place, such as a store or one's home. (From Western movies.) □ *I'm going next door to visit Mrs. Jones. You stay here and hold the fort.* □ *You should open the store at eight o'clock and hold the fort until I get there at ten o'clock.*

hold up one's end (of the bargain) See hold one's end (of the bargain) up.

Hold your horses! Slow down! Don't be so eager! □ *MARY: Come on, Sally, let's get going! SALLY: Oh, hold your horses! Don't be in such a rush!* □ *"Hold your horses!" said Fred to the group of small boys trying to get into the station wagon.*

home in on something to go toward a specific place; to aim toward or be directed toward a specific thing or place and move directly toward it. □ *The missile homed in on the target.* □ *The tired athlete homed in on the finish line.*

a **hop, skip, and a jump** a short distance. □ *Bill lives just a hop, skip, and a jump from here. We can be there in two minutes.* □ *My car is parked just a hop, skip, and a jump away.*

a **horse of a different color** See a horse of another color

a **horse of another color** AND **a horse of a different color** another matter altogether. □ *I was talking about the tree, not the bush. That's a horse of another color.* □ *Gambling is not the same as investing in the stock market. It's a horse of a different color.*

How about a lift? See Could I have a lift?

How about that! Isn't that amazing!; How surprising! □ *The plane left the gate early. How about that!* □ *How about that! The Cubs won the World Series!*

How dare you! It is incredible that you should even try to do such a thing!; I am shocked and angered that you would (even) suggest doing such a thing! □ *How dare you! You cannot speak to me that way!* □ *Don't touch me again! How dare you!*

huff and puff to breath very hard; to pant as one exerts effort. □ *John came up the stairs huffing and puffing.* □ *He huffed and puffed and finally got up the steep hill.*

hunger for something to have a strong desire for something. □ *All her life, Mary has hungered for affection.* □ *The prisoner hungered for freedom.*

hungry for something desiring someone or something. □ *The orphan was hungry for the warmth of a family.* □ *Bill is hungry for knowledge and is always studying.*

hurl an insult (at someone) to direct an insult at someone; to say something insulting directly to someone. □ *Anne hurled an insult at Bob that made him very angry.* □ *If you two would stop hurling insults, we could have a serious discussion.*

Hurry on! Keep going!; Move faster! □ *TOM: Get going! Hurry on! SUE: I'm hurrying as fast as I can.* □ *MARY: Hurry on! CHILD: I can't go any faster!*

a **hush fell over someone or something** [for silence] to envelop someone or something. □ *As the conductor raised his arms, a hush fell over the audience.* □ *The coach shouted and a hush fell over the locker room.*

hustle and bustle very busy or frenzied activity and confusion. □ *I can't stand the hustle and bustle of big cities.* □ *There is a lot of hustle and bustle in this office at the end of the fiscal year.*

I beg your pardon. 1. I am very sorry and I apologize. □ *I beg your pardon. I didn't mean to step on your toe.* □ *I beg your pardon. We seem to have bumped into each other.* **2.** What have you done?; How dare you!; What do you mean by that? (Usually **I beg your pardon!**) □ *I beg your pardon! You are sitting in my seat!* □ *I beg your pardon! I was here first!*

I can only do so many things at once. Don't be impatient with me, because I am already doing several things.; Please give me time to do what I have to do. □ *I will bring your coffee as soon as I can. I can only do so many things at once.* □ *I can't finish the typing today. I can only do so many things at once.*

(I'd) better get on my horse. an expression indicating that it is time that one departed. (Casual and folksy.) □ *JOHN: It's getting late. Better get on my horse. RACHEL: Have a safe trip. See you tomorrow.* □ *"I'd better get on my horse. The sun'll be down in an hour," said Tom, sounding like a cowboy.*

I didn't catch the name. AND **I didn't catch your name.** I don't remember your name.; I didn't hear your name when we were introduced. □ *BILL: How do you like this weather? BOB: It's not too good. By the way, I didn't catch your name. I'm Bob Wilson. BILL: I'm Bill Franklin. BOB: Nice to meet you, Bill.* □ *BOB: Sorry, I didn't catch the name. BILL: It's Bill, Bill Franklin. And you? BOB: I'm Bob Wilson.*

I didn't catch your name. See I didn't catch the name.

I didn't know you cared. I didn't know that you had tender feelings for me. □ *Flowers! How sweet! I didn't know you cared.* □ *I am amazed that you feel that way about me. I didn't know you cared.*

(I) don't believe I've had the pleasure. I believe I haven't met you yet. (A polite way of asking for an introduction.)

□ TOM: *I'm Tom Thomas. I don't believe I've had the pleasure.* BILL: *Hello. I'm Bill Franklin.* TOM: *Nice to meet you, Bill.* BILL: *Likewise.* □ BOB: *Looks like rain.* FRED: *Sure does. Oh, I don't believe I've had the pleasure.* BOB: *I'm Bob, Bob Jones.* FRED: *My name is Fred Wilson. Glad to meet you.*

I don't blame you. I understand how you feel and I do not fault you for feeling bad.; I am sympathetic with the way that you feel and what you intend to do. □ *I am sure that you are getting angry, and I don't blame you.* □ *I don't blame you for being upset.*

I don't have time to breathe. See I don't have time to catch my breath.

I don't have time to catch my breath. AND **I don't have time to breathe.** I am very busy.; I have been very busy. (See also time to catch one's breath. Compare with catch one's breath.) □ HENRY: *I'm so busy these days. I don't have time to catch my breath.* RACHEL: *Oh, I know what you mean.* □ SUE: *Would you mind finishing this for me?* BILL: *Sorry, Sue. I'm busy. I don't have time to breathe.*

I don't know about that! I think you are wrong!; I disagree with what you say or intend to do and will try to prevent it. □ *So, you plan to use my car? I don't know about that!* □ *Try to steal my purse, will you! I don't know about that! How do you like this pepper spray?*

I don't want to wear out my welcome. a phrase used by a guest who doesn't want to be a burden to the host or hostess by staying too long or by visiting too often. □ MARY: *Good night, Tom. You must come back again soon.* TOM: *Thank you. I'd love to. I don't want to wear out my welcome, though.* □ BOB: *We had a fine time. Glad you could come to our little gathering. Hope you can come again next week.* FRED: *I don't want to wear out my welcome, but I'd like to come again.* BOB: *Good. See you next week. Bye.* FRED: *Bye.*

if anything happens See if anything should happen.

if anything should happen AND **if anything happens** if a disaster happens. □ *I'll give you the phone number of my hotel, so you can reach me if anything happens.* □ *If anything should happen, I want you to look after my children.*

if I've told you once, I've told you a thousand times an expression that introduces a scolding, usually to a child. □ *MOTHER: If I've told you once, I've told you a thousand times, don't leave your clothes in a pile on the floor! BILL: Sorry.* □ *"If I've told you once, I've told you a thousand times, keep out of my study!" yelled Bob.*

if I were you an expression introducing a piece of advice. □ *JOHN: If I were you, I'd get rid of that old car. ALICE: Gee, I was just getting to like it.* □ *HENRY: I'd keep my thoughts to myself, if I were you. BOB: I guess I should be careful about what I say.*

if not if that is not [the case]; if that is not so; otherwise; if that does not happen. □ *I must leave here by 5:15. If not, I will miss my bus.* □ *He should be here at noon. If not, we will eat without him.*

if so if that is [the case]; if that is so. □ *She might be late. If so, we will eat without her.* □ *She is supposed to be all right. If so, we have nothing to worry about.*

if worst comes to worst in the worst possible situation; if things really get bad. (A cliché.) □ *If worst comes to worst, we'll hire someone to help you.* □ *If worst comes to worst, I'll have to borrow some money.*

if you ask me if you want my opinion; my opinion is as follows. □ *If you ask me, we pay enough taxes as it is.* □ *She spends too much time with that boy, if you ask me.*

If you can't lick 'em, join 'em. If you can't overcome or compete with some group, then it is best to join or seek to be like that group. (Here, *lick* means "beat" or "defeat.") □ *There are so many big cars on the road that I finally bought one myself. If you can't lick 'em, join 'em.* □ *So, you went to work for the biggest company in town. Well, if you can't lick 'em, join 'em, I guess.*

if you know what's good for you if you know what will work to your benefit; if you know what will keep you out of trouble. □ *MARY: I see that Alice has put a big dent in her car. SUE: You'll keep quiet about that if you know what's good for you.* □ *SALLY: My boss told me I had better improve my spelling. BILL: If you know what's good for you, you'd better do it, too.*

I hate to eat and run I regret just eating at this social event and then immediately leaving. (An apology made by someone who must leave a social event very soon after eating.) □ *I hate to eat* *and run, but I have to catch a plane early in the morning.* □ *We just hate to eat and run, but Jane has a headache.*

I hate to mention it I regret having to bring these facts to your attention. □ *I hate to mention it, but you owe me $100.* □ *I hate to mention it, but you are sitting in my chair.*

I haven't got all day. Be quick, because I'm in a hurry. □ *RACHEL: Make it snappy! I haven't got all day. ALICE: Just take it easy. There's no rush.* □ *HENRY: I haven't got all day. When are you going to finish with my car? BOB: As soon as I can.*

I haven't seen you in a month of Sundays. I haven't seen you in a long time. (Colloquial and folksy.) □ *TOM: Hi, Bill. Haven't seen you in a month of Sundays! BILL: Hi, Tom. Long time no see.* □ *BOB: Well, Fred! Come right in! I haven't seen you in a month of Sundays! FRED: Good to see you, Uncle Bob.*

I hear what you're saying. AND **I hear you. 1.** I know exactly what you mean!; I think the same thing! □ *JOHN: The prices in this place are a bit steep. JANE: Man, I hear you!* □ *BILL: I think it's about time for a small revolution! ANDREW: I hear what you're saying.* **2.** an expression indicating that one has heard and understood someone's statement, but implying that one does not agree. □ *TOM: The time has come to do something about that ailing dog of yours. MARY: I hear what you're saying. I just don't intend to do what you think I should do.* □ *JANE: It would be a good idea to have the house painted. JOHN: I hear what you're saying, but I'm concerned about the cost.*

I hear you. See I hear what you're saying.

I hope you are proud of yourself! You should have known better than to behave in that way, and I hope you feel ashamed of yourself. (Sarcastic.) □ *You made her cry. I hope you are proud of yourself!* □ *You certainly made a fool of yourself in the meeting. I hope you are proud of yourself!*

I (just) don't get it. I simply don't understand this matter.; I don't understand this issue. □ *I've tried to understand it, but I just don't get it.* □ *I don't get it. He keeps making the same mistake.*

I kid you not. I am not kidding you.; I am not trying to fool you. □ *BILL: Whose car is this? SALLY: It's mine. It really is. I kid you not.* □ *"I kid you not," said Tom, glowing. "I outran the whole lot of them."*

I know just how you feel! I sympathize with your feelings!; I would feel the same way if I were you! (Both physical and emotional feelings.) □ *You must be very upset after the argument. I know just how you feel.* □ *What a terrible day! I know just how you feel!*

I know the feeling. I know how you feel because I have experienced the same thing. (Both physical and emotional feelings.) □ *You are upset about losing your job. I know the feeling.* □ *I know the feeling. When you stay up very late at night, you just can't stand to wake up early in the morning.*

I'll be hanged! I am totally surprised! (Informal.) □ *You got a new car! Well, I'll be hanged!* □ *I'll be hanged! Billy passed algebra!*

I'll bite. Okay, I will answer your question.; Okay, I will listen to your joke or play your little guessing game. □ *BOB: Guess what is in this box. BILL: I'll bite. BOB: A new toaster!* □ *JOHN: Did you hear the joke about the used car salesman? JANE: No, I'll bite.*

ill-disposed to doing something not friendly; not favorable; not well disposed. □ *I am ill-disposed to doing hard labor.* □ *The police chief was ill-disposed to discussing the details of the case with the news reporters.*

ill-gotten gains money or other possessions acquired in a dishonest or illegal fashion. □ *Bill cheated at cards and is now living on his ill-gotten gains.* □ *Mary is enjoying her ill-gotten gains. She deceived an old lady into leaving her $5,000 in her will.*

I'll have to beg off. a polite expression used to turn down an informal invitation. □ *ANDREW: Thank you for inviting me, but I'll have to beg off. I have a conflict. HENRY: I'm sorry to hear that. Maybe some other time.* □ *BILL: Do you think you can come to the party? BOB: I'll have to beg off. I have another engagement. BILL: Maybe some other time.*

I'll let you go. It is time to end this phone conversation. □ *Well, I'll let you go. It's getting late.* □ *I have to go to work early tomorrow, so I'll let you go.*

I'll thank you to keep your opinions to yourself. I do not care about your opinion of this matter. □ *JANE: This place is sort of drab. JOHN: I'll thank you to keep your opinions to yourself.* □ *BILL: Your whole family is sort of long-legged. JOHN: I'll thank you to keep your opinions to yourself.*

ill will hostile feelings or intentions. □ *I hope you do not have any ill will toward me because of our argument.* □ *Dave felt such ill will toward his family that he left his fortune to his best friend.*

Imagine that! I am so surprised to hear that!; I could hardly even imagine that, because it is so strange or wonderful. □ *The teachers all went on strike. Imagine that!* □ *John and Mary are going to Tahiti. Imagine that!*

I'm cool. I'm fine. (Slang.) □ *BOB: How you been? FRED: I'm cool, man. Yourself? BOB: The same.* □ *FATHER: How are you, son? BILL: I'm cool, Dad. FATHER (misunderstanding): I'll turn up the heat.*

I'm easy. I am very easy to please. (Informal.) □ *Don't worry about me. I'll sit anywhere. I'm easy.* □ *I'll eat whatever no one else wants. I'm easy.*

I'm just looking. See I'm only looking.

I'm just minding my own business. an answer to an inquiry about what one is doing. (This answer also can carry the implication "Since I am minding my own business, why aren't you minding your own business?" Compare with Mind your own business.) □ *TOM: Hey, man, what are you doing? BILL: Minding my own business. See you around.* □ *SUE: Hi, Mary. What have you been doing? MARY: I'm just minding my own business and trying to keep out of trouble.*

I'm off. an expression said by someone who is just leaving. (Slang.) □ *BOB: Time to go. I'm off. MARY: Bye.* □ *SUE: Well, it's been great visiting. Good-bye. Got to go. MARY: I'm off, too. Bye.*

I'm only looking. AND **I'm just looking.** I am not a buyer, I am only examining your merchandise. (A phrase said to a shopkeeper or clerk who asks, "May I help you?") □ *CLERK: May I help you? MARY: No, thanks. I'm only looking.* □ *CLERK: May I help you? JANE: I'm just looking, thank you.*

implicate someone (in something) to suggest that someone is involved in something. □ *The mayor was implicated in the murder.* □ *Jane's essay implicated her teacher in the cheating scandal.*

I'm (really) fed up (with someone or something). I have had enough of someone or something, and something must be done. □ *TOM: This place is really dull. JOHN: Yeah. I'm fed up with it.*

I'm leaving! □ *SALLY: Can't you do anything right? BILL: I'm really fed up with you! You're always picking on me!*

I'm sorry. an expression used to excuse oneself politely or to apologize, especially when one has collided with someone, when one has offended someone, or to ask someone to repeat what has been said. □ *"I'm sorry," I said to the woman I had just bumped into.* □ *I'm sorry, what did you say? I couldn't hear you.*

in abeyance in reserve. □ *Until the judge determined that the evidence could be used in the trial, it was held in abeyance.* □ *I kept my opinion in abeyance.*

in a bind in a difficult situation. □ *I was really in a bind when I lost my job.* □ *You really got in a bind when you quit your job.*

in a (constant) state of flux See in flux.

in a dead heat finishing a race at exactly the same time; tied. (Here, *dead* means "exact" or "total.") □ *The two horses finished the race in a dead heat.* □ *They ended the contest in a dead heat.*

in advance [of something given, paid, or provided] before it is due. □ *The bill isn't due for a month, but I paid it in advance.* □ *I want my pay in advance.*

in a fix in an awkward situation. □ *I was in a real fix because I'd made two dates for the same night.* □ *Every time Dave was in a fix, he called his mother for help.*

in a flash quickly; immediately. □ *I'll be there in a flash.* □ *It happened in a flash. Suddenly my wallet was gone.*

in agreement in harmony; agreeing. □ *The managers were all in agreement about marketing strategies.* □ *Because Bob and Bill were never in agreement, they were always bickering.*

in a haze in a state of confusion. □ *After being hit in the head by the bat, Bill was in a haze.* □ *After surgery, I was in a haze until the anesthetic wore off.*

in a huff in an angry or offended manner. (*In* can be replaced with *into*. See the examples.) □ *He heard what we had to say, then left in a huff.* □ *She came in a huff and ordered us to bring her something to eat.* □ *She gets into a huff very easily.*

in a jiffy in a brief moment; in a short period of time. □ *I'll be there in a jiffy. Just wait for me.* □ *I'll be finished with this small job in a jiffy.*

in a little bit in a small amount of time. □ *I will be there in a little bit. Please wait.* □ *In a little bit, we can go outside and play.*

in all my born days as long as I have been alive. (Informal.) □ *I have never heard of any such thing in all my born days!* □ *In all my born days, I never dreamed I would see so much money!*

in a mad rush in a great hurry. □ *I ran around all day today in a mad rush, looking for a present for Bill.* □ *Why are you always in a mad rush?*

in a nutshell [of news or information] in a (figurative) capsule. □ *This cable channel provides the latest news in a nutshell.* □ *In a nutshell, what happened at work today?*

in a pinch 1. as a substitute. □ *A piece of clothing can be used as a bandage in a pinch.* □ *In a pinch, you can use folded paper to prop up the table leg so the table won't rock.* **2.** in an awkward situation where help is needed and alternatives do not exist. □ *I'm sort of in a pinch. Can you give me some help?* □ *If you are ever in a pinch, just ask me for help.*

in arrears [of debts] overdue. □ *Jane's student loan payments are in arrears.* □ *The accounts of the bankrupt company were in arrears.*

in a rut See stuck in a rut.

in a stupor in a dazed condition; in a condition in which one cannot concentrate or think. □ *The drunk driver walked away from the car accident in a stupor.* □ *In the morning, Mary remains in a stupor until she drinks coffee.*

in behalf of someone AND **on behalf of someone** representing someone; speaking for someone. □ *The actor's agent accepted the award in behalf of her client.* □ *The club president spoke on behalf of the committee.*

in between located in the middle of two things. □ *It is not hot or cold. It's in between.* □ *A sandwich consists of two slices of bread with some other food in between.*

in bloom AND **in blossom** with many flowers; at the peak of blooming. □ *The garden is beautiful when it is in bloom.* □ *The roses are in blossom, and they smell so sweet!*

in blossom See in bloom.

in bulk in large quantities or amounts, rather than smaller, more convenient quantities or amounts. □ *Jane always bought office supplies in bulk to save money.* □ *Dave purchased cereal in bulk because his family used so much of it.*

in case in the event that . . . ; to prepare for the possibility that . . . □ *What do we do in case the building catches fire?* □ *We should close all of the windows just in case it rains.*

in case of something if a problem occurs; if something happens; in the event that something happens. □ *What do we do in case of fire?* □ *In case of an accident, call the police.*

inclined to do something tending to do something; leaning toward doing something. □ *Tom is inclined to tell jokes when he is with a group of people.* □ *I'm inclined to go to the beach tomorrow if it doesn't rain.*

in contempt (of court) considered to have shown disrespect for a judge or for courtroom procedures. □ *The bailiff ejected the lawyer who was held in contempt.* □ *The judge found the juror in contempt of court when she screamed at the attorney.*

incumbent (up)on someone to do something obligatory for someone to do something. □ *It is incumbent upon me to inform you that you are up for review.* □ *It was incumbent on Mary to mail her application before June 1.*

in custody in the condition of being kept guarded by police. □ *The suspect was in custody awaiting a trial.* □ *How long has the prisoner been in custody?*

in debt having debts; having much debt; owing money. □ *Mary is deeply in debt.* □ *I am in debt to the bank for my car loan.*

in denial in a state of refusing to believe something that is true. □ *Mary was in denial about her illness and refused treatment.* □ *Tom doesn't think he's an alcoholic because he's still in denial.*

in detail including lots of details; giving all the details. □ *I explained the policy to the customer in detail.* □ *We planned the entire project in great detail.*

in disguise hidden behind a disguise; looking like something else. □ *Santa Claus was really the little child's father in disguise.* □ *What I thought was terrible turned out to be a blessing in disguise!*

in drag in the clothing of the opposite sex. (Usually refers to a man wearing women's clothing.) □ *The actor played the woman's part in drag.* □ *We all went to the costume party dressed in drag.*

in earnest with sincerity. □ *I spent the day writing the paper in earnest.* □ *Mary's comments were in earnest. She really meant them.*

in effect producing a particular effect, even if not producing it directly; virtually. □ *In effect, this new law will raise taxes for most people.* □ *This policy harms domestic manufacturers. In effect, all our clothing will be made in foreign countries.*

in existence now existing; currently and actually being. □ *The tiger may not be in existence in a few decades.* □ *All the oil in existence will not last the world for another century.*

in fact truly; actually. □ *I wasn't in California last week. In fact, I've never been there.* □ *In fact, you should never have asked the question.*

in fashion fitting in well with the clothing that has been designed for a particular season of a particular year; currently considered stylish. □ *I understand that long skirts are in fashion this year.* □ *I always want to find out what styles are in fashion so I can avoid them.*

in flight while flying; while on an airplane that is flying. □ *A passenger became ill in flight, and the pilot had to return to the airport.* □ *I really don't care to eat in flight. I am too nervous.*

in flux AND **in a (constant) state of flux** in constant change; changing. □ *I can't describe my job because it's in a constant state of flux.* □ *The price of gold is in flux.*

in general referring to the entire class being discussed; speaking of the entire range of possibilities; in most situations or circumstances. □ *I like vegetables in general, but not beets.* □ *In general, I prefer a hotel room on a lower floor, but I will take a higher room if it's special.*

in hand controlled; under control. □ *I thought I had my destiny in hand, but then fate played a trick on me.* □ *Don't worry about me. I have everything in hand.*

in heaven in a state of absolute bliss or happiness. □ *Lisa was in heaven after winning the lottery.* □ *Resting in his hammock, John was simply in heaven.*

in hock in debt. □ *After buying the luxury car, Bob was in hock for years.* □ *I am deeply in hock and have to pay off my debts.*

in horror with intense shock or disgust. □ *Mike stepped back from the rattlesnake in horror.* □ *The jogger recoiled in horror when she came upon a body in the park.*

in ink written or signed with a pen that uses ink. □ *You should write your report in ink.* □ *You must sign your checks in ink.*

in its entirety AND **in their entirety** totally; including all of something. □ *I watched the basketball game in its entirety.* □ *My friends and I ate the two large pizzas in their entirety.*

in jeopardy in danger; at risk; at hazard. □ *John puts himself in jeopardy every time he goes skydiving.* □ *I was in jeopardy when my car broke down on the deserted road.*

in labor [of a woman] experiencing the pains and exertion of childbirth. □ *Susan was in labor for nearly eight hours.* □ *As soon as she had been in labor for an hour, she went to the hospital.*

in league (with someone) [of people] secretly cooperating, often to do something bad or illegal. □ *The county sheriff is in league with criminals.* □ *The car thieves and the police are in league to make money from stolen cars.*

in limbo in a state of uncertainty. □ *My scholarship is in limbo until Congress finalizes the budget.* □ *After our huge argument, our wedding date was in limbo.*

in line in a line or row of people waiting for something. □ *How long have you been standing in line?* □ *We waited in line for an hour to buy tickets.*

in many respects See in some respects.

in memory of someone to continue the good memories of someone; for the honor of a deceased person. □ *Many highways were* *renamed in memory of John F. Kennedy.* □ *We planted roses in memory of my deceased father.*

in midair at a point high in the air. □ *The planes crashed in midair.* □ *Extra fuel was released from the plane in midair.*

in my opinion See as I see it.

in my view See as I see it.

in need [of someone] requiring basic things like food, clothing, and housing. □ *Please contribute some money for those who are in need.* □ *The charity works with elderly people who are in need.*

in need of something [of someone or some creature] requiring something. □ *We are in need of a new car.* □ *The company is in need of a larger building to hold all its employees.*

in neutral with the shift lever of a vehicle in the position where the motor is running but is not engaging the wheels or other moving parts. □ *The car rolled down the hill because I'd left it in neutral.* □ *If you are moving and in neutral, you do not have control of your vehicle.*

in one fell swoop [accomplishing much] in one swift action. □ *In one fell swoop, management laid off 800 workers.* □ *The bear managed to capture two large fish in one fell swoop.*

in park [of an automobile transmission] having the gears locked so the automobile cannot move. □ *The driver stopped the car and placed it in park.* □ *You have to be in park in order to start this car.*

in pencil written or signed with a pencil. □ *Why did you write your report in pencil?* □ *You can't sign a check in pencil!*

in perpetuity for an indefinitely long period of time. □ *The right for the road to cross my land was granted in perpetuity to the county.* □ *This memorial will remain in perpetuity to honor our fallen heroes.*

in person [of people] actually present in a place rather than appearing in a film, on a television screen, or through a radio broadcast. □ *All the famous movie stars were there in person.* □ *You must appear at the office in person to collect the money that is due to you.*

in place of someone or something instead of someone or something; as a substitute for someone or something. □ *I changed my mind. I want a red one in place of the blue one.* □ *John came to help in place of Max, who was sick.*

in practice in real life; concerning actual events, as opposed to just talk or thinking. □ *In practice, some of our policies are overlooked.* □ *In theory, my boss should do this job, but in practice, he doesn't.*

in progress under way; happening; developing or moving right now. □ *Don't enter the studio. There's a show in progress.* □ *We now return you to the regularly scheduled program already in progress.*

in proportion AND **out of proportion** showing the right or wrong proportion relative to something else. □ *That dog's large head is out of proportion to its small body.* □ *The cartoonist drew the dog in proportion to its surroundings.*

in public in such a place or such a way that other people can see or know about something. □ *It's illegal to walk naked in public.* □ *John always tries to embarrass me whenever we're in public.*

in reality viewing things realistically; really; actually. □ *Jane dreamed it was snowing, but in reality, it was very warm.* □ *John looks happy, but in reality, he is miserable.*

in receipt of something in a state of having received something. □ *We are in receipt of your letter of request.* □ *When we are in receipt of your check for the full balance, we will mark your bill as paid.*

in recent memory in the recent past; during the period of time in which things happened that can still be remembered. □ *Never in recent memory has there been this much snow!* □ *Our school has only won the contest once in recent memory.*

in rehearsal at a particular stage of development in the production of a play, opera, or concert when there are many rehearsals. □ *The play is in rehearsal now and will open next month.* □ *While the opera was still in rehearsal, the star developed a hatred for the director.*

in remission [of a serious disease] not as bad as it was and seeming to be getting better. □ *While the disease was in remission,*

John got to leave the hospital. □ *The doctor says my cancer is in remission.*

in retrospect reconsidering the past with the knowledge one now has. □ *In retrospect, I would have gone to a better college.* □ *David realized, in retrospect, that he should have married Jane.*

in return by way of giving something back; as a way of paying someone back for something; as part of an exchange. □ *I helped Tom yesterday, and he helped me in return today.* □ *I paid $20 and received four tickets in return.* □ *If you are very kind to people, often they will be very kind to you in return.*

in ruin in a state of having been destroyed. □ *The enemy army left each town that it attacked in ruin.* □ *The crops lay in ruin after the flood.*

in secret secretly. □ *The terrorists planned in secret to blow up the bridge.* □ *I will tell Mary about the party in secret so no one else will hear.*

in session [of a court, congress, or other organization] operating or functioning. □ *Smoking is forbidden while the meeting is in session.* □ *The spectators must remain very quiet while court is in session.*

in seventh heaven in a very happy state. (A cliché. This is the highest heaven, where God exists.) □ *Anne was really in seventh heaven when she got a car of her own.* □ *I'd be in seventh heaven if I had a million dollars.*

in shambles in a messy state; destroyed. □ *After the earthquake, the town lay in shambles.* □ *The TV set was in shambles after John tried to fix it.*

in shape [of someone] in good physical condition. □ *I exercise regularly to stay in shape.* □ *I am not in shape, and I cannot run far without panting.*

in short supply scarce. (*In* can be replaced with *into*. See the examples.) □ *Fresh vegetables are in short supply in the winter.* □ *Red cars are in short supply because everyone likes them and buys them.* □ *At this time of the year, fresh vegetables go into short supply.*

in sight able to be seen; within the range of one's vision. □ *I hear birds, but there are none in sight.* □ *The locusts ate everything in sight.*

in someone's behalf See on someone's behalf.

in some respects AND **in many respects** with regard to some or many details. □ *In some respects, Anne's comments are similar to yours.* □ *The three proposals are quite different in many respects.*

in spite of someone or something without regard to someone or something; even though another course has been prescribed; ignoring a warning. □ *In spite of her orders to stay, I left.* □ *In spite of the bad weather, I had fun on vacation.*

in storage in a place where things are stored or kept. □ *Mary placed her winter clothes in storage during the summer.* □ *John's furniture is in storage while he is in the army.*

in surgery performing or undergoing surgery. □ *Dr. Smith is in surgery now.* □ *The patient is still in surgery.*

in tandem in single file. □ *We marched to the door in tandem.* □ *They rode along in tandem.*

in tatters in torn pieces of cloth. □ *The poor man's clothes hung in tatters.* □ *The flag was in tatters after the storm.*

intent on doing something determined to do something. □ *The children were intent on making a snowman.* □ *The prisoner was intent on escaping.*

in terms of something relating to something; with regard to something. □ *In terms of value to this company, how much do you think you are worth?* □ *Is this a good paint job on my car—in terms of the quality, not the color?*

in the affirmative in the form of an answer that means yes. □ *The soldier answered in the affirmative by nodding his head "yes."* □ *My manager's response was in the affirmative.*

in the context of something in the circumstances under which something happens. □ *In the context of a funeral, laughing loudly is inappropriate.* □ *In the context of an argument, it is fine to speak firmly.*

in the event of something if something happens; on the chance that something happens. □ *In the event of his late arrival, please call me.* □ *In the event of rain, the parade will be canceled.*

in the forefront (of something) See at the forefront (of something).

in the interim (between things) in the meantime; in the time between the end of something and the beginning of something else. □ *In the interim between her morning and afternoon classes, Susan rushed home to get a book she had forgotten.* □ *My favorite show starts in five minutes, but I'll talk to you in the interim.*

in their entirety See in its entirety.

in the laundry with the clothes that are waiting to be washed. □ *Is my blue shirt clean or is it in the laundry?* □ *All my socks are in the laundry. What shall I do?*

in the mainstream (of something) following the current trends or styles that are popular or are considered normal. □ *Bob is too old-fashioned to be in the mainstream of modern living.* □ *Max likes to make fun of people in the mainstream.*

in the market for something ready and eager to buy something. □ *I am in the market for a new car. Are there any good deals right now?* □ *Bill is in the market for a new suit.*

in the meantime in the period of time between two things; within the period of time between now and when something is supposed to happen. □ *The movie starts at six o'clock. In the meantime, let's eat dinner.* □ *My flight is not until 8:27. In the meantime, I will read a book.*

in the mood for something AND **in the mood to do something** having the proper state of mind for a particular situation or for doing something. □ *I'm not in the mood to see a movie tonight.* □ *Are you in the mood for pizza?*

in the mood to do something See in the mood for something.

in the neighborhood of something See somewhere in the neighborhood of something.

in the nude in a state of nudity; having no clothes on. □ *Bill says he sleeps in the nude.* □ *All the little boys swam in the nude in the creek.*

in the open in the outdoors; in an area that is not closed in. □ *John's bike was stolen because he left it out in the open.* □ *Mary loves gardening because she loves to be in the open.*

in theory according to a theory; theoretically. □ *In theory, if I take my medicine regularly, I will get well.* □ *How things work in theory doesn't always match how they work in reality.*

in the rear located in the space or area behind someone or something. □ *The waiter told me that the bathrooms were in the rear.* □ *All deliveries must be made in the rear.*

in the trust of someone under the responsibility of someone; in the care of someone. □ *The state placed the orphan in the trust of the foster parents.* □ *Our bonds are left in the trust of our broker.*

in this day and age now; in these modern times. □ *BILL: Ted flunked out of school. MOTHER: Imagine that! Especially in this day and age.* □ *BILL: Taxes keep going up and up. BOB: What do you expect in this day and age?*

in time before the deadline; before the time limit; within the allotted period of time; soon enough [for something or to do something]. □ *I hope we get there in time to go swimming before dark.* □ *Am I in time for the cake and ice cream?*

in times past long ago; in previous times. □ *In times past, you would not have been able to wear casual clothing to work.* □ *In times past, the air always seemed fresher and cleaner.*

in(to) a jam in(to) a difficult situation. □ *Mary cannot keep track of the many times Dave has gotten himself into a jam.* □ *I found myself in a jam when my car overheated on the highway.*

into being into existence. □ *The new law brought more problems into being.* □ *That idea came into being centuries ago.*

in(to) someone's clutches in(to) the control of someone who has power or authority over someone else. □ *Snow White fell into the clutches of the evil witch.* □ *Once you're in my clutches, I'll ruin you.*

in tow closely following; under someone's control. □ *The nanny walked into the park with three children in tow.* □ *The manager went to the meeting with her staff in tow.*

in transit in the process of being transported. □ *Dave is in transit from London to Chicago.* □ *The new computer is now in transit from the manufacturer.*

in triplicate produced in three copies. □ *Mr. Smith asked me to type up his notes in triplicate.* □ *I completed each form in triplicate.*

in trouble in danger; at risk. □ *If you don't be quiet, you're going to be in trouble.* □ *The company was in trouble for months and then went bankrupt.*

in tune AND **out of tune** in or out of a state where musical notes are at their proper intervals so that none are flat or sharp. □ *Your piano is out of tune.* □ *The choir members all sang in tune.*

in turn at the appropriate point in a series or an order; when one's turn comes. □ *Someone has to wash the dishes after every meal. All of us will have to do it in turn.* □ *All three of them shared the task of carrying water in turn.*

invasion of one's privacy an intrusion that results in the loss of one's privacy. □ *Your invasion of my privacy is not welcome!* □ *The athlete complained about the invasion of his privacy by the press.*

invest someone's time in something to put one's time, effort, or energy into a project. □ *Mary invests her time in charity work.* □ *I invested five weeks of my time building this model ship.*

invest someone with something to endow someone with something, such as a power or privilege. □ *The constitution invests the vice president with the power to act on behalf of the president in certain conditions.* □ *The state has invested me with the authority to unite this couple in marriage.*

invest something in someone or something to place power under the control of someone or something. □ *The constitution has invested certain powers in the federal government and left the rest to the states.* □ *The law invests the power to arrest criminals in the sheriff's department.*

invite someone to resign to fire someone. (A euphemism.) □ *The board of trustees has invited me to resign.* □ *I quit before my boss had a chance to invite me to resign.*

I owe you one. I appreciate what you did, and now I owe you a favor. □ *BOB: I put the extra copy of the book on your desk. SUE:*

Thanks, I owe you one. □ BILL: *Let me pay for it.* BOB: *Thanks a lot, I owe you one.*

I read you loud and clear. 1. a response, used by someone communicating by radio, stating that one understands the previous transmission clearly. (*Read* is in the present tense.) □ *CONTROLLER: This is Aurora Center, do you read me? PILOT: Yes, I read you loud and clear.* □ *CONTROLLER: Left two degrees. Do you read me? PILOT: Roger. Read you loud and clear.* **2.** I understand what you are telling me. (Used in general conversation, not in radio communication.) □ *BOB: Okay. Now, do you understand exactly what I said? MARY: I read you loud and clear.* □ *MOTHER: I don't want to have to tell you again. Do you understand? BILL: I read you loud and clear.*

issue a call for something to make an invitation or request for something. □ *The prime minister issued a call for peace.* □ *The person who organized the writing contest issued a call for entries.*

(It) beats me. AND **(It's) got me beat.; You got me beat.** I do not know the answer.; I cannot figure it out.; The question has me stumped. (In the main entry, the stress is on *me*.) □ *BILL: When are we supposed to go over to Tom's? MARY: Beats me.* □ *SALLY: What's the largest river in the world? BOB: You got me beat.*

It blows my mind! It really amazes and shocks me. (Slang.) □ *BILL: Did you hear about Tom's winning the lottery? SUE: Yes, it blows my mind!* □ *JOHN: Look at all that paper! What a waste of trees! JANE: It blows my mind!*

It just goes to show (you) (something). That incident or story has an important moral or message. □ *TOM: The tax people finally caught up with Henry. SALLY: See! It just goes to show.* □ *Indignant over the treatment she received at the grocery and angry at the youthful clerk, Sally muttered, "Young people. They expect too much. It just goes to show you how society has broken down."*

It's business as usual. Things will continue to function as they have in the past, regardless of what has happened. □ *Yes, there is a terrible storm raging outside, but in here it is business as usual.* □ *At our house, we are all very busy. Despite the fact that three of us are still sick, it's business as usual.*

(It's) got me beat. See (It) beats me.

It's just not my day! Everything seems to be going wrong for me! □ *I just broke a fingernail. It's just not my day.* □ *I did it wrong again! It's just not my day!*

It's not supposed to. AND **Someone's not supposed to.** a phrase indicating that someone or something is not meant to do something. (Often with a person's name or a pronoun as a subject. See the examples.) □ *FRED: This little piece keeps falling off. CLERK: It's not supposed to.* □ *BILL: Tom just called from Detroit and says he's coming back tomorrow. MARY: That's funny. He's not supposed to.*

It's not the end of the world. This is not the worst thing that can happen.; It is not as bad as it may seem. □ *Yes, you lost your job, but it's not the end of the world.* □ *Don't yell at the baby for spilling his milk. It's not the end of the world.*

it strikes me that . . . it seems to me that . . . □ *HENRY: It strikes me that you are losing a little weight. MARY: Oh, I love you!* □ *"It strikes me that all this money we are spending is accomplishing very little," said Bill.*

It's your funeral. If that is what you are going to do, you will have to endure the consequences. □ *TOM: I'm going to call in sick and go to the ball game instead of to work today. MARY: Go ahead. It's your funeral.* □ *BILL: I'm going to take my car to the racetrack and see if I can race against someone. SUE: It's your funeral.*

It's your move. 1. [in a game] You should make the next game play or move. □ *It's your move. Keep playing so we can finish this game.* □ *I played before the telephone call interrupted us, so now it's your move.* **2.** You have to do the next thing. □ *She asked you the question, so it's your move.* □ *Tom insulted you, and it's your move. I suggest ignoring him.*

(I've) been keeping cool. AND **(I've been) keeping cool.** an answer to a question about what one has been doing during very hot weather. (Without *I've*, this can also be used as a question.) □ *JANE: How do you like this hot weather? BILL: I've been keeping cool.* □ *MARY: Been keeping cool? BOB: Yeah. I have the air conditioning on full blast.*

I've been keeping myself busy. a typical response to an inquiry about what one has been doing. □ *BILL: What have you been doing? BOB: I've been keeping myself busy. What about you? BILL:*

About the same. □ *JOHN: Yo! What have you been up to? BILL: I've been keeping myself busy.*

I've been keeping out of trouble. a response to any inquiry that asks what one has been doing. □ *JOHN: What have you been doing, Fred? FRED: I've been keeping out of trouble. JOHN: Yeah. Me too.* □ *MARY: How are things, Tom? TOM: Oh, I've been keeping out of trouble.*

I've been up to no good. a vague response indicating that one has been doing mischief. □ *JOHN: What have you been doing, Tom? TOM: Oh, I've been up to no good, as usual. JOHN: Yeah. Me too.* □ *MARY: Been keeping busy as usual? SUE: Yeah. I've been up to no good. MARY: I should have known.*

I've got it! I have discovered it!; I have figured out the answer!; I have a solution to the problem. □ *I've got it! The butler committed the crime.* □ *I've got it! The answer is 2,343,523.*

I've got to fly. See I've got to run.

I've got to go home and get my beauty sleep. a phrase announcing one's need to depart. (As if getting plenty of sleep is part of what one does to make oneself more beautiful. Used especially when one is leaving some place or some event in the evening or at night.) □ *SUE: Leaving so early? JOHN: I've got to go home and get my beauty sleep.* □ *JANE: I've got to go home and get my beauty sleep. FRED: Well, you look to me like you've had enough. JANE: Why, thank you.*

I've got to run. AND **I've got to fly.; I've got to split.; I've got to take off.** a phrase announcing one's need to depart. □ *MARY: Want to watch another movie? BILL: No, thanks. I've got to run.* □ *JANE: Look at the time! I've got to fly. MARY: See you later, Jane.* □ *BILL: It's getting late. I've got to split. SUE: Okay, see you tomorrow. BILL: Good night.* □ *MARY: I've got to take off. Bye. BOB: Leaving so soon? MARY: Yes. Time to go. BOB: Bye.*

I've got to split. See I've got to run.

I've got to take off. See I've got to run.

I've heard that one before. That is an old joke, excuse, or story and I have heard it before. □ *So, the family dog ate your homework. I've heard that one before.* □ *I've heard that one before. In fact, it is the oldest joke I have ever heard.*

I've only got one pair of hands. I can't do all this work any faster. □ *I will get you your coffee in a minute. I only have one pair of hands.* □ *I can't get all this typing done today. I only have one pair of hands!*

(I was) just wondering. a comment made after hearing a response to a previous question. (See examples for typical patterns.) □ *JOHN: Do you always keep your film in the refrigerator? MARY: Yes, why? JOHN: I was just wondering.* □ *BOB: Did this cost a lot? SUE: I really don't think you need to know that. BOB: Sorry. Just wondering.*

I wouldn't dream of it! I certainly would not do, say, or think it! □ *Do you think I will complain about this to the police? I wouldn't dream of it!* □ *Let Tom borrow my car? I wouldn't dream of it!*

The **jig is up.** Everything is finished.; We have been found out.; You have been caught.; The plot or plan is spoiled. □ *The police are outside. The jig is up.* □ *The jig's up. The whole plan has been discovered.*

jog someone's memory to stimulate someone's ability to recall something. □ *Hearing the first part of the song I'd forgotten really jogged my memory.* □ *I tried to jog Bill's memory about our childhood antics.*

join forces to join together into a single large group. □ *Both parties joined forces to protest the tax increase.* □ *Our band joined forces with another band and gave a very exciting concert.*

join hands [for people] to hold hands so that each person is holding the hands of two other people; [for two people] to hold each other's hands. □ *Let us join hands and pray together.* □ *The dancers joined hands and formed a circle that moved to the left.*

join the fray AND **jump into the fray** to join the fight or argument. □ *After listening to the argument, Mary decided to jump into the fray.* □ *Tom joined the fray and immediately got knocked down.*

joking aside See all joking aside.

jolt to a start AND **jolt to a stop** to start or stop suddenly, causing a jolt. □ *The truck jolted to a stop at the stop sign.* □ *The little car jolted to a quick start and threw the passenger back in his seat.*

jolt to a stop See jolt to a start.

jump into the fray See join the fray.

just a minute only a short time; [wait] a short period of time. □ *I'll be there in just a minute!* □ *Could I have just a minute of your time?*

just between you and me as a secret that only you and I know. □ *I think—just between you and me—that the boss ought to retire.* □ *Just between you and me, this party is awfully dull.*

(just) squeak by to barely accomplish something. □ *"I just squeaked by on that history test!" John exclaimed.* □ *Mary just squeaked by on her budget this month.*

Just wondering. See I was just wondering.

keen on doing something willing or eager to do something. □ *Dave isn't very keen on going to the opera.* □ *The children are keen on swimming this afternoon. Shall I take them?*

keep a close rein on someone or something See keep a tight rein on someone or something.

keep an eye out (for someone or something) See have an eye out (for someone or something).

keep a secret to know a secret and not tell anyone. □ *Please keep our little secret private.* □ *Do you know how to keep a secret?*

keep a tight rein on someone or something AND **keep a close rein on someone or something** to watch and control someone or something diligently. □ *The office manager kept a tight rein on the staff.* □ *Mary keeps a close rein on her children.*

keep bankers' hours to work for less than eight hours a day. □ *The advertising agency keeps bankers' hours. It is only open until four.* □ *James doesn't really work full-time. He keeps bankers' hours.*

keep company to associate with or visit someone often. □ *Anne keeps company with many neighbors on her block.* □ *Bill and Mary have been keeping company a lot lately.*

keep from doing something to avoid doing something; to refrain from doing something. □ *How could I keep from crying? It was so sad!* □ *Try to keep from falling off the ladder.*

Keeping cool. See I've been keeping cool.

keep in touch (with someone or something) AND **remain in touch (with someone or something); stay in touch (with someone or something)** to maintain communications with someone; to maintain up-to-date knowledge about someone or something. □ *After my neighbor moved, we still remained in touch.* □ *I want to stay in touch with my office over the weekend.*

keep one's ear to the ground to listen carefully, hoping to get advance warning of something. □ *John kept his ear to the ground, hoping to find out about new ideas in computers.* □ *His boss told him to keep his ear to the ground so that he'd be the first to know of a new idea.*

keep one's eye on someone or something to watch someone or something carefully; to monitor someone or something. □ *Please keep your eye on the children while I go to the store.* □ *Bill kept an eye on his expenses because he was spending too much money.*

keep one's nose to the grindstone to work hard at one's job or task. □ *Keep your nose to the grindstone and you will succeed.* □ *If Tom had kept his nose to the grindstone, he would be a vice president by now.*

keep up (with the times) to stay in fashion; to keep up with the news; to be contemporary or modern. □ *I try to keep up with the times. I want to know what's going on.* □ *I bought a whole new wardrobe because I want to keep up with the times.* □ *Sally learns all the new dances. She likes to keep up.*

Keep your nose out of my business. See Mind your own business.

Keep your shirt on. Please be patient. (Informal.) □ *I'll open the door in a minute. Keep your shirt on!* □ *Keep your shirt on! I'll bring you your coffee in a minute! I've only got two hands!*

killed outright killed immediately. □ *The driver was killed outright in the accident.* □ *Twenty people were killed outright in the explosion. Five others died later of their injuries.*

kind of ＿＿＿ somewhat a certain way; having a small or noticeable amount of a characteristic; rather ＿＿＿; sort of ＿＿＿. □ *I am kind of tired. Let's go home.* □ *An orange can be kind of sweet and kind of sour at the same time.*

a **kind of something** a variety of something that is fairly close to the real thing, even though it is not exactly the real thing. □ *I used a folded newspaper as a kind of hat to keep the rain off.* □ *Bill is serving as a kind of helper or assistant on this project.*

known fact something that is generally recognized as a fact. □ *That grass is green is a known fact.* □ *It is a known fact that John was in Chicago on the night of the murder.*

known quantity someone or something whose characteristics are recognized and understood. □ *Lisa is a known quantity, and I am sure she will not surprise us by voting with the opposition.* □ *Jane's old car doesn't run very well, but at least it's a known quantity.*

know something in one's bones See feel something in one's bones.

know the score See know what's what.

know what's what AND **know the score** to know the facts; to know the facts about life and its difficulties. □ *Bob is so naive. He sure doesn't know the score.* □ *I know what you're trying to do. Oh, yes, I know what's what.*

lapse into a coma to go into a coma. □ *The survivor of the crash lapsed into a coma.* □ *Aunt Mary lapsed into a coma and died.*

the **last (one)** someone or something that is the final one in a sequence. □ *Anne was the last one to get concert tickets.* □ *This is the last of the artist's paintings. The artist finished it a week before she died.*

lay down one's life for something to die for something. □ *The soldier laid down his life for his country.* □ *She laid down her life for her children.*

lay someone off to inactivate a worker; to fire someone from a job. □ *The company laid off a thousand workers because there wasn't enough demand for their products.* □ *I hope they don't lay me off.*

lay someone to rest to bury a dead person. (A euphemism.) □ *They laid her to rest beside her mother and father, out in the old churchyard.* □ *We gather together today to lay our beloved son to rest.*

lay something to waste AND **lay waste to something** to destroy something (literally or figuratively). □ *The invaders laid the village to waste.* □ *The kids came in and laid waste to my clean house.*

lay waste to something See lay something to waste.

leading question a question that strongly suggests what kind of answer the person who asks it wants to hear. □ *The mayor was angered by the reporter's leading questions.* □ *"Don't you think that the police are failing to stop crime?" is an example of a leading question.*

lean toward doing something to tend toward doing something; to favor doing something. □ *The union is leaning toward accept-*

ing the proposal. □ *My friends leaned toward swimming instead of shopping.*

leave a sinking ship See desert a sinking ship.

leave one's mark on someone [for someone like a teacher] to affect the behavior and performance of another person. □ *The wise professor left her mark on her students.* □ *My father left his mark on me, and I will always remember all his good advice.*

lend someone a hand See give someone a hand.

lend (someone) a helping hand to assist someone with a task. □ *Mary lent a helping hand at the garage sale.* □ *I need someone to lend me a helping hand with this job.*

the **lesser (of the two)** the smaller one (of two); the one having the least amount. □ *The last two pieces of pie were not quite the same size, and I chose the lesser of the two.* □ *If you are offered two different amounts of money, you will certainly not choose the lesser.*

the **lesser of two evils** of a pair of bad things, the one that is less bad; the better of two bad options. □ *I didn't like either politician, so I voted for the lesser of two evils.* □ *Given the options of going out with someone I don't like and staying home and watching a boring television program, I chose the lesser of the two evils and watched television.*

let go of someone or something to release someone or something. □ *Please let go of me!* □ *Don't let go of the steering wheel.*

let out a sound to make [some kind of a] sound. □ *Be quiet. Don't let out a sound!* □ *Suddenly, Jane let out a shriek.*

Let's do lunch (sometime). See We('ll) have to do lunch sometime.

let someone go to fire someone. □ *They let Rita go from her job.* □ *I'm afraid we're going to have to let you go.*

let someone know (about something) to tell someone something; to inform someone of something. □ *Please let me know about it soon.* □ *Will you be coming to the picnic? Please let me know.*

let something pass to let something go unnoticed or unchallenged. □ *Bob let Bill's insult pass because he didn't want to argue.* □ *Don't worry, I'll let this little incident pass.*

let something slide (by) AND **let something slip (by) 1.** to forget or miss an important time or date. □ *I'm sorry I just let your birthday slip by.* □ *I let it slide by accidentally.* **2.** to waste a period of time. □ *You wasted the whole day by letting it slip by.* □ *We were having fun, and we let the time slide by.*

let something slip (by) See let something slide (by).

Let's shake on it. Let us mark this agreement by shaking hands. □ *BOB: Do you agree? MARY: I agree. Let's shake on it. BOB: Okay.* □ *BILL: Good idea. Sounds fine. BOB (extending his hand): Okay, let's shake on it. BILL (shaking hands with Bob): Great!*

let us do something [I suggest] we will or should do something [together]. □ *Let us go in peace.* □ *Let us bow our heads in prayer.*

level something at someone to aim a remark at someone; to direct something at someone. □ *John leveled a sarcastic comment at his teacher.* □ *The editorial leveled its remarks at the mayor.*

level with someone (about someone or something) to be straightforward with someone about something; to be sincere about someone or something. □ *The police encouraged the criminal to level with them about the crime.* □ *Level with me, and tell me what you thought of my cake.*

license to do something permission, right, or justification to do something. □ *You have no license to behave in that manner!* □ *Who granted you license to enter my house without knocking?*

a **lick of work** [not even] a bit of work. (Always expressed in the negative.) □ *I couldn't get her to do a lick of work all day long!* □ *The boys didn't do a lick of work while you were away.*

lie fallow 1. [for land] to remain unused. □ *Each year we let a different section of our farmland lie fallow.* □ *The land that is lying fallow this year will be cultivated next year.* **2.** [for a skill or talent] to remain unused and neglected. □ *You should not let your talent lie fallow. Practice the piano before you forget how to play it.* □ *His writing had lain fallow for so long that he could hardly write a proper sentence.*

lie in wait (for someone or something) to stay still and hidden, waiting for someone or something. □ *Bob was lying in wait for Anne so he could scold her about something.* □ *The assassin lay in wait for his target to approach.*

like blazes 1. very fast; like hell. □ *The deer ran like blazes to get away.* □ *The car sped by like blazes.* **2.** Oh, indeed!; That's what you think!; I don't believe what you are telling me! (Usually **Like blazes!** *Blazes* is a euphemism for *hell*.) □ *Like blazes! No such think ever happened!* □ *Like blazes I am the new president!*

like mad very intensely; very much. □ *Since I was very late, I drove down the highway like mad.* □ *I wrote like mad, trying to meet my deadline.*

the **likes of someone or something** anyone or anything similar to someone or something; the equal or equals of someone or something. □ *I never want to see the likes of you again!* □ *We admired the splendid old ships, the likes of which will never be built again.*

litmus test a question or experiment that seeks to determine the state of one important factor. (Also used literally for a test of acidity using a special substance called "litmus.") □ *His performance on the long exam served as a litmus test to determine whether he would go to college.* □ *The amount of white cells in my blood became the litmus test for diagnosing my disease.*

live a life of something to have a life of a certain quality or style. □ *The movie star lived a life of luxury.* □ *After Anne won the lottery, she lived the life of a queen.*

Long time no see. I have not seen you in a long time.; We have not seen each other in a long time. □ *TOM: Hi, Fred. Where have you been keeping yourself? FRED: Good to see you, Tom. Long time no see.* □ *JOHN: It's Bob! Hi, Bob! BOB: Hi, John! Long time no see.*

look down on someone or something to look upon someone or something with dislike or scorn. □ *Bob looks down on me for not having my own car.* □ *They look down on us because we are poor.*

lose one's mind to become crazy or insane; to become irrational. □ *If I don't get some sleep, I'm going to lose my mind.* □ *All this extra work is going to make me lose my mind!*

lose one's temper (at someone or something) to become angry at someone or something. □ *Lisa lost her temper and began shouting at Bob.* □ *I hate to lose my temper at someone. I always end up feeling guilty.*

lose one's train of thought to forget what one was talking about. □ *ANDREW: I had something important on my mind, but that telephone call made me lose my train of thought. MARY: Did it have anything to do with money, such as the money you owe me? ANDREW: I can't remember.* □ *TOM: Now, let's take a look at, uh . . . well . . . next I want to talk about something that is very important. MARY: I think you lost your train of thought. TOM: Don't interrupt. You'll make me forget what I'm saying.*

lose track (of someone or something) to lose contact with someone; to forget where something is. □ *I lost track of all my friends from high school.* □ *Tom has lost track of his glasses again.*

a **lot of** AND **lots of** a large number of people or things; much of something. □ *I got a lot of presents for my birthday.* □ *I ate lots of pizza for dinner.*

lots of See lot of.

Lovely weather for ducks. a greeting phrase meaning that this unpleasant rainy weather must be good for something. □ *BILL: Hi, Bob. How do you like this weather? BOB: Lovely weather for ducks.* □ *SALLY: What a lot of rain! TOM: Yeah. Lovely weather for ducks. Don't care for it much myself.*

lower oneself to some level to bring oneself down to some lower level or behavior. □ *I refuse to lower myself to your level.* □ *Has TV news lowered itself to the level of the tabloids?*

lull before the storm a quiet period just before a period of great activity or excitement. □ *It was very quiet in the cafeteria just before the students came in for lunch. It was the lull before the storm.* □ *In the brief lull before the storm, the clerks prepared themselves for the doors to open and let in thousands of shoppers.*

lull someone into a false sense of security to lead someone into believing that all is well before attacking or doing something bad. □ *We lulled the enemy into a false sense of security by pretending to retreat. Then we launched an attack.* □ *A strong economy lulled us into a false sense of security, and we were not prepared when the banks failed.*

lull someone to sleep to cause someone to fall asleep. □ *The mother lulled her baby to sleep.* □ *The boring professor lulled the students to sleep.*

mad about someone or something AND **mad for someone or something** having a strong interest in someone or something; very enthusiastic about someone or something. □ *I'm absolutely mad for strawberry cheesecake.* □ *Anne and Bill are mad about ballroom dancing.*

mad for someone or something See mad about someone or something.

make a break for something to make a sudden rush toward something. □ *When it started raining, we made a break for shelter.* □ *The cat made a break for the door when it was opened.*

make a friend AND **make friends** to establish a link of friendship with someone. □ *I have never found it difficult to make friends.* □ *Mary had to make new friends when she changed schools.*

make a living by doing something See make a living from something.

make a living from something AND **make a living by doing something** to earn a living from something or by doing something. □ *John makes a living from painting houses.* □ *Can you really make a living by designing jewelry?*

make allowances for someone to make excuses for someone's behavior. □ *You make too many allowances for your children's bad behavior.* □ *I have to make allowances for John. He hasn't been well lately.*

make allowances for something to keep something in mind when making a decision or policy. □ *I will have to make allowances for the possibility of an extra guest at dinner.* □ *The company made no allowances for bad weather in its attendance policy.*

make amends (for something) to do something as an act of restitution or to make up for some error, injury, or loss that one has caused. □ *The day after the argument, Jane called her friend to make amends.* □ *After amends had been made, John took his friend to dinner.*

make a pass at someone to attempt to flirt with someone; to offer unwanted sexual invitations to someone. □ *John made a pass at the woman sitting next to him at the bar.* □ *Mary did not want to dance with the man who had made a pass at her.*

make (both) ends meet to earn and spend equal amounts of money. □ *I have to work at two jobs to make ends meet.* □ *Through better budgeting, I am learning to make both ends meet.*

make friends See make a friend.

make fun of someone or something to tease and make jokes about someone or something; to ridicule someone; to mock someone or something. □ *Please don't make fun of my dog!* □ *Jimmy cries when people make fun of him.*

make it to succeed; to realize a goal. □ *If you don't study, you'll never make it.* □ *Bill was proud that he made it on his own without anyone's help.*

make it worth someone's while to provide something, such as a bribe or a reward, that makes it beneficial for someone to do something. □ *I made it worth the waiter's while to give us good service.* □ *If you'll throw a few contracts my way, I'll make it worth your while.*

Make my day! See Go ahead, make my day!

make overtures to give hints about something; to present or suggest ideas. □ *The company made overtures about hiring me.* □ *Tom is making overtures about inviting us to his country home next month.*

make someone's gorge rise to cause someone to become very angry. □ *The unnecessary accident made my gorge rise.* □ *Getting his tax bill made Bob's gorge rise.*

make someone's head spin 1. to make someone dizzy or disoriented. □ *Riding in your car makes my head spin.* □ *Breathing the gas made my head spin.* **2.** to confuse or overwhelm someone. □ *All these numbers make my head spin.* □ *The physics lecture made my head spin.*

make something up to create a story or a lie. □ *That's not true! You just made it up!* ⊺ *Bob made up a story about a tiny mouse and its friends.*

make up for something to give recompense for something; to provide enough of something to balance a lack of it. □ *Here is a cup of sugar to make up for the one that I borrowed.* □ *I hope this money makes up for the damage I did to your car.*

make up (with someone) to reconcile with someone; to end a disagreement (with someone). □ *Bill and Max decided to make up.* □ *They made up with each other and are still very good friends.*

make use of someone or something to use or utilize someone or something. □ *If you make use of all your talents and skills, you should succeed.* □ *The technician makes good use of a number of special tools.*

a **marked man** someone who is in danger of harm by someone else. (Usually with males.) □ *Bob's a marked man. His teacher found out that he's been missing lectures.* □ *Fred's a marked man, too. Mary is looking for him to get her money back from him.*

a **marvel to behold** someone or something quite exciting or wonderful to see. □ *Our new house is a marvel to behold.* □ *Mary's lovely new baby is a marvel to behold.*

a **match for someone or something** someone or some creature that is the equal of someone or some other creature, especially in a contest. □ *My older brother is no match for me; he's much weaker.* □ *Your horse is no match for mine in a race. Mine will always win.*

mean (for someone) to do something to intend (for someone) to do something. □ *John meant to go with us to the zoo.* □ *Tom meant for Jane to do the dishes.*

meant to be destined to exist. □ *Our love was meant to be!* □ *It was not meant to be.*

meant to be something destined or fated to be something. □ *Jane was meant to be a chemist.* □ *I was meant to be rich, but something didn't work right!*

meeting of minds the establishment of agreement; complete agreement. □ *After a lot of discussion, we finally reached a meeting of* *minds.* □ *We struggled to bring about a meeting of minds on the issues.*

meet one's death AND **meet one's end** to experience something, especially death or problems. □ *After 20 years, my dog finally met his death when he got hit by a bus.* □ *The sky diver met his end when his parachute didn't open.*

meet one's end See meet one's death.

mention someone or something in passing to mention someone or something while talking about something else. □ *He just happened to mention in passing that the mayor had resigned.* □ *John mentioned in passing that he was nearly eighty years old.*

milk someone for something to pressure someone into giving information or money. □ *The reporter milked the mayor's aide for information.* □ *The thief milked me for twenty dollars.*

mince (one's) words to soften the effect of one's words. □ *Tell me what you think, and don't mince your words.* □ *A frank person never minces words.*

Mind if I join you? See Could I join you?

mind your manners to be careful to use good manners. □ *Remember to mind your manners while we are visiting Aunt Mary's house.* □ *Jimmy! Mind your manners!*

Mind your own business. AND **Get your nose out of my business.; Keep your nose out of my business.** Stop prying into my affairs. (Not at all polite. The expressions with *get* and *keep* can have the literal meanings of removing and keeping removed. Compare with I'm just minding my own business.) □ *ANDREW: This is none of your affair. Mind your own business. SUE: I was only trying to help.* □ *BOB: How much did you pay in federal taxes last year? JANE: Good grief, Bob! Keep your nose out of my business!* □ *TOM: How much did it cost? SUE: Tom! Get your nose out of my business!* □ *"Hey!" shrieked Sally, jerking the checkbook out of Sue's grasp. "Get your nose out of my business!"*

the **minute something happens** the point in time at which an event happens. □ *I'll be inside the minute it rains.* □ *Call me the minute you get to town.*

misplace one's trust (in someone) to put trust in the wrong person; to put trust in someone who does not deserve it. □ *The* *writer misplaced his trust in his editor.* □ *The voters misplaced their trust in the corrupt politician.*

mission in life one's purpose for living; the reason for which one is on the earth. □ *Bob's mission in life is to make money.* □ *My mission in life is to help people live in peace.*

a **mixed bag** a varied collection of people or things. □ *The new pupils are a mixed bag—some bright, some positively stupid.* □ *The furniture I bought is a mixed bag. Some of it is valuable and the rest is worthless.*

monkey around to fool around; to misbehave. □ *If you don't stop monkeying around, I'm going to leave.* □ *John monkeyed around while he was supposed to be working.*

monkey (around) with something to tamper or tinker with something. □ *I monkeyed with the antenna because the TV reception was bad.* □ *Don't monkey around with my computer while I'm on vacation.*

monkey business activities that are peculiar or out of the ordinary, especially mischievous or illegal ones. □ *There's been some monkey business in connection with the firm's accounts.* □ *Bob left the firm quite suddenly. I think there was some monkey business between him and the boss's wife.*

months running See days running.

more and more an increasing amount; additional amounts. □ *As I learn more and more, I see how little I know.* □ *Dad seems to be smoking more and more lately.*

murder on something very destructive or harmful to something. □ *Running a marathon is murder on your knees.* □ *This dry weather is murder on my crops.*

muster (up) one's courage to build up one's courage; to call or bring forth one's courage. □ *I mustered my courage and dove from the high diving board.* □ *He had to muster up all his courage in order to attend the dance.*

My lips are sealed. I will tell no one this secret or this gossip. □ *MARY: I hope you don't tell anyone about this. ALICE: Don't worry. My lips are sealed.* □ *BOB: Don't you dare tell her I told you. BILL: My lips are sealed.*

needle in a haystack something that is hopelessly lost. □ *Trying to find a white dog in the snow is like looking for a needle in a haystack.* □ *I tried to find my lost contact lens on the beach, but it was like looking for a needle in a haystack.*

neither does someone [does] not either. □ *Susan does not own a cat, and neither does Mary.* □ *Bill doesn't want to see a movie tonight, and neither do I.*

Never fear! Do not worry!; Be confident that everything will be all right!; Trust me! □ *Never fear! I will be on time.* □ *Tom will do the assignment. Never fear!*

new blood a new and energetic person; new and energetic people. □ *The company fired some employees and hired new blood.* □ *A little new blood on the committee wouldn't hurt.*

new hire a person who has recently been hired; a newly employed person. □ *Anne is our new hire who will begin work Tuesday.* □ *The accounting department is full of new hires.*

next-door neighbor the person living in the house or apartment closest to one's own. □ *My next-door neighbor came over to borrow a shovel.* □ *I will be visiting our next-door neighbor, so if you need me, you can find me there.*

next of kin someone's closest living relative or relatives. □ *The police notified the dead man's next of kin.* □ *My next of kin lives 800 miles away.*

next to nothing hardly anything; almost nothing. □ *This car is worth next to nothing. It's full of rust.* □ *I bought this antique chair for next to nothing.*

next to someone or something near to someone or something; adjacent to someone or something. □ *I live next to a bank.* □ *Please sit next to me.*

nice and _____ having enough of some quality; adequately a certain way; sufficiently some way. □ *It is nice and cool this evening.* □ *I think your steak is nice and done now. If I cook it any longer, it will be overcooked.*

nip in the air a cold feeling; coldness. □ *I felt a nip in the air when I opened the window.* □ *There's more of a nip in the air as winter approaches.*

No dice! No!; Absolutely not! □ *You want me to take the test for you? No dice!* □ *No dice! I refuse to do it!*

No hard feelings. There is no feeling of insult, abuse, resentment, or hurt. □ *I understand that you meant no harm. No hard feelings.* □ *It was an accident. I am sorry. No hard feelings?*

no skin off someone's nose no difficulty for someone; no concern of someone. (A cliché.) □ *It's no skin off my nose if she wants to act that way.* □ *She said it was no skin off her nose if we wanted to sell the house.*

no spring chicken getting old; old. □ *That actress is no spring chicken, but she does a pretty good job of playing a twenty-year-old girl.* □ *JANE: How old do you think Robert is? JILL: Well, he's certainly no spring chicken.*

Not a bit. Not at all.; No feeling or response at all. □ *Am I worried? Not a bit.* □ *Of course, I am not upset. Not a bit.*

not able to stomach someone or something AND **cannot stomach someone or something** not to be able to put up with someone or something; not to be able to tolerate or endure someone or something. □ *Jane cannot stomach violent movies.* □ *We were not able to stomach their rude behavior.*

not a kid anymore getting old; old. □ *You can't keep partying all weekend, every weekend. You're not a kid anymore.* □ *KATHY: Bill is just as wild as ever, I hear. JANE: Bill needs to realize that he's not a kid anymore.*

not as young as one used to be getting old; old. □ *Aunt Lila isn't as young as she used to be. She can't take a lot of trips anymore.* □ *Don't walk so fast! I'm not as young as I used to be. It takes me a while to catch up.*

Not by a long shot. Not at all.; Certainly not.; Definitely not. (The stress is on *long*.) □ *His work is not satisfactory. Not by a long shot.* □ *You are not finished with the assignment. Not by a long shot.*

not for hire [of a taxi] not available to take new passengers. □ *The taxi was going to pick someone up at a nearby hotel and was not for hire.* □ *The taxi had a lighted sign that said it was not for hire.*

not going to win any beauty contests ugly. □ *Fred isn't going to win any beauty contests, but he's smart and considerate and very successful at his job.* □ *This old truck of mine is not going to win any beauty contests, but I wouldn't trade it for anything.*

no thanks to you I cannot thank you for what happened, because you did not cause it.; I cannot thank you for your help, because you did not give it. □ *BOB: Well, despite our previous disagreement, he seemed to accept all our demands. ALICE: Yes, no thanks to you. I wish you'd learn to keep your big mouth shut!* □ *JANE: It looks like the picnic wasn't ruined despite the fact that I forgot the potato salad. MARY: Yes, it was okay. No thanks to you, of course.*

[not] have anything to do with someone or something See have nothing to do with someone or something.

Not if I can help it. Not if I can do anything to prevent it. □ *He will not sell the house! Not if I can help it!* □ *We won't be late. Not if I can help it.*

Not if I see you first. See Not if I see you sooner.

Not if I see you sooner. AND **Not if I see you first.** a response to "I'll see you later." (This means you will not see me if I see you first, because I will avoid you. Often used jokingly.) □ *TOM: See you later. MARY: Not if I see you sooner.* □ *JOHN: Okay. If you want to argue, I'll just leave. See you later. MARY: Not if I see you first.*

Not in my book. Not according to my views. □ *JOHN: Is Fred okay for the job, do you think? MARY: No, not in my book.* □ *SUE: My meal is great! Is yours a real winner? BOB: Not in my book.*

not know when one is well off not to know that one is in a good situation. □ *Poor Tom doesn't know when he is well off. He always thinks other people are luckier than he is.* □ *I should be happy about it. I guess I don't know when I am well off.*

not one's cup of tea not something one prefers. □ *Playing cards isn't her cup of tea.* □ *Sorry, that's not my cup of tea.*

not one's place not one's role to do something. □ *It was not my place to criticize my boss.* □ *It was Bill's place to ask the questions, not yours.*

Not on your life! No, absolutely not! □ *SALLY: Do you want to go downtown today? BILL: Not on your life! There's a parade this afternoon.* □ *SUE: I was cheated out of fifty dollars. Do you think I need to see a lawyer? JOHN: Not on your life! You'll pay more than that to walk through a lawyer's door.*

Not so fast! Do not reach a conclusion so fast!; Don't attempt to leave so quickly or so soon.; Don't be in such a hurry to do something. □ *Not so fast! Don't leave without saying good-bye.* □ *Not so fast! We need to talk this over.*

Not (too) much. a response to inquiries into what one has been doing. □ *JOHN: What have you been doing? MARY: Not much.* □ *SUE: Been keeping busy? What are you up to? BOB: Not too much.*

not up to snuff not adequate. □ *Sorry, your paper isn't up to snuff. Please do it over again.* □ *The performance was not up to snuff.*

not with it not able to think clearly; not able to understand things. □ *Lisa's mother is not really with it anymore. She's becoming senile.* □ *Tom's not with it yet. He's only just come around from the anesthetic.*

now and then sometimes; occasionally. □ *I like to go to a movie now and then.* □ *We visit my parents now and then, but we never have a real vacation.*

null and void without legal force; having no legal effect. □ *The judge declared the law to be null and void.* □ *The millionaire's will was null and void because it was unsigned.*

a **number of things or people** some things or people, in an indefinite amount; several or many things or people. (In this expression, *number* is treated as plural.) □ *I subscribe to a number of magazines.* □ *A number of people have recommended this movie.*

nurse someone back to health [for anyone] to provide medical care and other help that gradually restores someone to good health. □ *After my operation, my mother nursed me back to health.*

□ *Mary nursed him back to health with plenty of good food and loving care.*

nuzzle up to someone or something to nestle against someone or something, especially if leading with the nose or face. □ *The puppy nuzzled up to its mother.* □ *Tom nuzzled up to Jane and asked her for a kiss.*

an **ocean of someone or something** See oceans of someone or something.

oceans of someone or something AND an **ocean of someone or something** a very large amount of something; a very large number of people or things. □ *The naughty student was in oceans of trouble.* □ *After a week of vacation, there was an ocean of work to do.* □ *The actor became nervous when he looked at the audience and saw an ocean of people watching him.*

the **odd something** an occasional item or object; just one or a few of something, not a large number or a full set. □ *In addition to adjusting the size of the jacket, the tailor repaired the odd loose button on the front.* □ *When I travel, I might buy the odd trinket or two, but I never spend much money.*

off campus not located on the grounds of a college or university. □ *Tom has an apartment off campus.* □ *The dean is off campus and cannot be reached.*

off chance slight possibility. □ *I need your phone number on the off chance I need more help.* □ *There's an off chance that we might be hiring next month.*

Off we go. We are just now leaving.; Let us leave now.; Here we go. (Also with other personal pronouns.) □ *Off we go. We have to catch our bus.* □ *It's time to leave. Off we go.* □ *Good-bye. Off I go.*

of interest (to someone) interesting to someone. □ *This is no longer of any interest.* □ *This is of little interest to me.*

an **old hand at doing something** someone who is experienced at doing something. □ *The maid was an old hand at polishing silver.* □ *Bob is an old hand at training dogs.*

on a lark See for a lark.

on a shoestring using or having a very small amount of money. □ *We lived on a shoestring for years before I got a good job.* □ *John traveled to Florida on a shoestring.*

on a splurge having a brief period of extravagance, especially extravagant spending. □ *Bob went on a splurge and bought a new car.* □ *Susan has been on another spending splurge! Look at that new furniture.*

on balance See all in all.

on behalf of someone See in behalf of someone.

on Broadway located in the Broadway theater district in New York City; currently performing or being performed in the Broadway theater district. □ *Our musical is the best thing on Broadway!* □ *I want to be a star on Broadway someday.*

on campus located or being on the grounds of a college or university. □ *Do you live on campus or off campus?* □ *I don't think that Lisa is on campus right now.*

on consignment [of goods] having been placed in a store for sale, without transferring the title of the goods to the operator of the store. □ *The artist placed his work in a gallery on consignment.* □ *I will attempt to sell your clothing on consignment.*

on credit using credit; buying something using credit. □ *I tried to buy a new suit on credit, but I was refused.* □ *The Smiths buy everything on credit and are very much in debt.*

one final thing See one final word.

one final word AND **one final thing** a phrase introducing a parting comment or the last item in a list. □ *JOHN: One final word, keep your chin up. MARY: Good advice!* □ *SUE: And one final thing, don't haul around a lot of expensive camera stuff. It just tells the thieves who to rob. JOHN: There are thieves here? SUE: Yeah. Everywhere.*

One never knows. A person can never know the full story.; Many things are in doubt and unexplainable. □ *She might have won the election. One never knows.* □ *One never knows. Things may change someday.*

one of these (fine) days sometime, possibly when one leasts expects it. □ *One of these fine days you will find that your new* *house isn't big enough any longer.* □ *I will win the lottery one of these fine days.*

one's bag of tricks a collection of special techniques or methods. □ *What have you got in your bag of tricks that could help me with this problem?* □ *Here comes Mother with her bag of tricks. I'm sure she can help us.*

one's bread and butter someone's livelihood or income. (The source of money that puts bread and butter, or other food, on the table.) □ *Selling cars is a lot of hard work, but it's my bread and butter.* □ *It was hard to give up my bread and butter, but I felt it was time to retire.*

one's heart goes out to someone to feel great sympathy for someone. □ *My heart goes out to the grieving family.* □ *Let your heart go out to those who are suffering, and pray for their improvement.*

one's heart is in one's mouth See under have one's heart in one's mouth.

one's sunset years one's old age. □ *Many people in their sunset years love to travel.* □ *Now is the time to think about financial planning for your sunset years.*

one thing or person after another a series of things or people that seems without limit. □ *It's just one problem after another.* □ *One customer after another has been buying shoes today!*

on fire burning; being burned with flames. □ *Help! My car is on fire!* □ *That house on the corner is on fire!*

on foot [running or walking] using the feet. □ *My car won't work so I have to travel on foot.* □ *We go everywhere on foot.*

on good terms (with someone) friendly with someone; able to interact well and be friends with someone. □ *Bill is on good terms with the people he works with.* □ *We are not on very good terms and don't speak to each other much.*

on hold the state a person or a telephone call is in when one remains connected to a telephone line while one's call has been temporarily suspended. □ *John is away from his desk. Let me put you on hold and find him.* □ *I waited on hold for three minutes, and then I hung up.*

on horseback on the back of a horse. □ *Anne rode on horseback across the field.* □ *Because they loved horses, the couple decided to marry on horseback.*

on impulse after having had an impulse or thought. □ *On impulse, Bob decided to buy a car.* □ *I didn't need a cellular telephone. I just bought it on impulse.*

on land on the soil; on the land and not at sea or in the air. □ *The flight was rough, and I feel better now that I am back on land.* □ *When I am at sea, I feel more relaxed than when I am on land.*

on location in or to a place—distant from the movie studio— where a movie is being filmed. □ *This movie was shot on location in Ontario.* □ *The actress went on location in Spain for her latest film.*

on occasion occasionally; sometimes; now and then. □ *I like to go to the movies on occasion.* □ *On occasion, Mary would walk her dog through the park.*

on one's own independently. □ *Our baby can now walk on his own.* □ *I have lived on my own since I was eighteen.*

on one's person [of something] carried with one. □ *Always carry identification on your person.* □ *I'm sorry, I don't have any money on my person.*

on one's way (to something or some place) See on the way (to something or some place).

on parole See out on parole.

on patrol See out on patrol.

on probation 1. serving a period of probation. □ *While Anne was on probation, she reported to her caseworker regularly.* □ *John was on probation for a year.* **2.** serving a trial period. □ *All new members are on probation for a year.* □ *I was on probation in my job for a full year before it became permanent.*

on purpose intentionally; in a way that is meant or intended; not by accident. □ *The bully stepped on my foot on purpose.* □ *Jimmy was jealous and destroyed Billy's sandcastle on purpose.*

on sale available for sale at a reduced price. □ *These pots are on sale for $20.* □ *I bought these pants on sale for half price.*

on someone's behalf AND **in someone's behalf** as a help to someone; to the benefit of someone. (Compare with in behalf of someone.) □ *A donation was made in the victim's behalf.* □ *Please don't do any extra work on my behalf.*

on someone's head [for something negative] to belong only to one person or group. □ *All the blame fell on their heads.* □ *I don't think that all the criticism should be on my head.*

on standby waiting for one's turn; ready and waiting for an opportunity to do something. (Especially used to describe the status of travelers who wait near a train, plane, or bus, hoping that a seat will become available.) □ *The passenger waited on standby for an available seat.* □ *The agent was able to seat all of the passengers who were on standby.*

on the bandwagon joined with others in supporting someone or something. □ *Come join us! Climb on the bandwagon and support Senator Smith!* □ *Look at all those people getting on the bandwagon! They don't know what they are getting into!*

on the bias on a diagonal line; on a diagonal pathway or direction. □ *The panels of the dress were cut on the bias.* □ *The seamstress sewed the fabric on the bias.*

on the borderline in an uncertain position between two statuses; undecided. □ *Bill was on the borderline between an A and a B in biology.* □ *Jane is on the borderline. She might succeed, or she might fail.*

on the defensive overly ready to defend oneself. □ *John goes on the defensive when his athletic ability is questioned.* □ *The child was on the defensive when questioned about cheating.*

on the level honest; dependably open and fair. (Also with *strictly.*) □ *How can I be sure you're on the level?* □ *You can trust Sally. She's strictly on the level.*

on the lookout for someone or something to watch carefully for someone or something that might be dangerous. □ *The campers were on the lookout for brown bears.* □ *The police were on the lookout for the escaped criminal.*

on the right track following the right set of assumptions. □ *Tom is on the right track and will solve the mystery soon.* □ *You are on the right track to find the answer.*

on the up and up honest and legal. (Usually used in the negative.) □ *I am not sure that Bill's business is entirely on the up and up.* □ *Stay away from that car dealer. She isn't exactly on the up and up.*

on the verge of (doing) something at the very beginning of doing something; just about to do something. □ *Bill was on the verge of leaving town when he found a job.* □ *Susan was on the verge of laughter, so she left the lecture hall.*

on the waiting list [for someone's name to be] on a list of people waiting for an opportunity to do something. (*The* can be replaced with *a*.) □ *I couldn't get a seat on the plane, but I got on a waiting list.* □ *There is no room for you, but we can put your name on the waiting list.*

on the way (to something or some place) AND **on one's way (to something or some place)** moving toward a place; advancing toward a new status or condition. □ *Is he here yet, or is he still on the way?* □ *Mary is better now and on her way to recovery.*

on time before the deadline; by the stated time. □ *Please make sure that your essays are completed on time.* □ *My taxes were not done on time, so I had to pay a penalty.*

an **open book** someone or something that is easy to understand. □ *Jane's an open book. I always know what she is going to do next.* □ *The council is an open book. It just wants to save money.*

open for business [of a shop, store, restaurant, etc.] operating and ready to do business. □ *The store is now open for business and invites you to come in.* □ *The construction will be finished in March, and we will be open for business in April.*

opening gambit an opening movement or statement which is made to secure a position that is to one's advantage. □ *The rebel army's opening gambit was to bomb the city's business district.* □ *The prosecution's opening gambit was to call a witness who linked the defendant to the scene of the crime.*

open to something agreeable to hearing or learning about new ideas and suggestions. □ *The store owner was open to suggestions from her employees.* □ *We are always open to new ideas.*

order of the day something necessary or usual at a certain time. □ *Warm clothes are the order of the day when camping in the* *winter.* □ *Going to bed early was the order of the day when we were young.*

or else or suffer the consequences. □ *Do what I tell you, or else.* □ *Don't be late for work, or else!*

the **other place** hell. (A euphemism.) □ *If you're good, you'll go to heaven, and if you're bad, you'll go to the other place.* □ *If she keeps up her drinking and gambling, she's headed to the other place for sure.*

out of control unrestrained; not manageable; disorderly. (Compare with under control.) □ *We called the police when things got out of control.* □ *The children are out of control and need to be disciplined.*

out of earshot too far from the source of a sound to hear the sound. □ *I was out of earshot and could not hear the conversation.* □ *Mary waited until her children were out of earshot before mentioning the party to Bill.*

out of one's head AND **out of one's mind; out of one's senses** silly and senseless; crazy; irrational. □ *Why did you do that? You must be out of your mind!* □ *Good grief, Tom! You have to be out of your head!* □ *She's acting as if she were out of her senses.*

out of one's mind See out of one's head.

out of one's senses See out of one's head.

out of proportion See in proportion.

out of spite with the desire to harm someone or something. □ *Jane told some evil gossip about Bill out of spite.* □ *That was not an accident! You did it out of spite.*

out of style no longer fashionable or stylish; not suitable as a current style. □ *Your clothes always look out of style!* □ *His ideas about teaching are out of style, but they are still good ideas.*

out of tune See in tune.

(out) on parole out of prison, conditionally, before one's total sentence is served. □ *Bob was caught using drugs while out on parole and was sent back to prison.* □ *He has to be careful and obey the law because he is out on parole.*

(out) on patrol away from a central location, watching over a distant area. □ *Officer Smith is out on patrol and cannot see you now.*

□ *The soldiers who are on patrol on this snowy night must be very cold.*

over again See all over again.

over and over repeatedly; again and again. □ *He repeated the sentence over and over until he had it memorized.* □ *She will practice it over and over until she can do it perfectly.*

over there See way over there.

owing to because of something; due to the fact of something. □ *Owing to the lateness of the evening, I must go home.* □ *We were late owing to the heavy traffic.*

pack of lies a series of lies. ☐ *The thief told a pack of lies to cover up the crime.* ☐ *John listened to Bill's pack of lies about the fight and became very angry.*

pal around with someone to spend a lot of time with someone; to do things with someone who is a friend. ☐ *Anne's husband still pals around with his college friends.* ☐ *Mary palled around with her girlfriend at the mall.*

palm something off (on someone) to try to get something accepted as good. ☐ *The crook palmed a fake $50 bill off on me.* ☐ *Bob palmed his research off as original work, but we all knew he plagiarized it.*

a **paradise (on earth)** a place on earth that is as lovely as paradise. ☐ *The retirement home was simply a paradise on earth.* ☐ *The beach where we went for our vacation was a paradise.*

partially sighted not able to see well. ☐ *Jane is partially sighted, but she is not able to see well enough to drive.* ☐ *I am not blind. I am partially sighted.*

partial to someone or something favoring or preferring something. ☐ *The boys think their teacher is partial to female students.* ☐ *I am partial to strawberry ice cream.*

the **particulars of something** specific details about something. ☐ *My boss stressed the important particulars of the project.* ☐ *What are the particulars of your request?*

pass away to die. (A euphemism.) ☐ *Mary's father passed away last week.* ☐ *When John passes away, he wants to be cremated.*

passport to something something that allows something good to happen. ☐ *John's new girlfriend is his passport to happiness.* ☐ *Anne's new job is a passport to financial security.*

patch something up [for people] to settle a quarrel and become friends again. □ *Bill and I patched up our little quarrel and had a cup of coffee together.* □ *The friends quickly patched up their disagreement.*

pay a call on someone to visit someone. □ *Grandmother always paid a call on us on Sundays.* □ *Let's pay a call on Mary at the hospital.*

pay attention (to someone or something) to give attention (to someone or something). □ *Please pay attention to the teacher.* □ *Max always pays careful attention to what is being told to him.*

pay a visit to someone or something See pay (someone or something) a visit.

pay for something to be punished for something. □ *John paid for his crime by going to jail for five years.* □ *The judge said that the thief would have to pay for her crimes.*

pay homage to someone to praise, respect, and honor someone. □ *My parents taught me to pay homage to my elders.* □ *The widower paid homage to his dead wife by placing flowers on her grave.*

pay one's debt to society to serve a prison sentence. □ *I've paid my debt to society, and I'm ready to be a responsible person.* □ *You can't hold Harry's crime against him forever. He paid his debt to society.*

pay one's last respects to attend the wake or funeral of someone; to approach the coffin containing someone in a final act of respect. □ *I went to Bill's wake to pay my last respects.* □ *Everyone in town came to the mayor's funeral to pay their last respects.*

pay someone a compliment to give someone a compliment. □ *Tom paid Bill a compliment when he told him he was intelligent.* □ *Mary was very gracious when Anne paid her a compliment.*

pay (someone or something) a visit AND **pay a visit to someone or something** to visit someone or something. □ *Bill paid a visit to his aunt in Seattle.* □ *Please pay a visit to our house whenever you are in town.* □ *Let's pay John a visit when we go to New York.*

pay someone respect to honor someone; to have and show respect for someone. □ *You really should pay your boss more respect.* □ *We have to pay our parents a lot of respect.*

pay to do something to be beneficial to do something; to be profitable. □ *It doesn't pay to drive downtown when you can take the train.* □ *It pays to take an umbrella with you if it's supposed to rain.*

peg someone as something AND **have someone pegged as something** to think of someone in a certain way. □ *Susan pegged the new employee as a lazy worker.* □ *I had you pegged as an angry rebel before I got to know you.*

per head See head.

persist in doing something to continue doing something. □ *John persists in thinking that he's always right.* □ *Tom persists in demanding that I agree to his terms.*

persist with something to continue the state of something; to extend an action or state. □ *Please do not persist with your demands that I agree to your terms.* □ *If you persist with this intrusion, I'm going to call the police.*

perspective on something the ability to look at a situation and determine what is important. □ *You don't have much perspective on this situation because you're so closely involved. The problem isn't really as serious as you think it is.* □ *Studying history gives one perspective on the past.*

pet hate something that is disliked intensely and is a constant or repeated annoyance. □ *My pet hate is being put on hold on the telephone.* □ *Another pet hate of mine is having to stand in line.*

pet peeve a frequent annoyance; one's "favorite" or most often encountered annoyance. □ *My pet peeve is someone who always comes into the theater after the show has started.* □ *Drivers who don't signal are John's pet peeve.*

pick a lock to open a lock without using a key. □ *The robber picked the lock with a nail file.* □ *The thief picked the lock on the safe and stole the money.*

the **pick of something** the best of the group. □ *This playful puppy is the pick of the whole lot.* □ *These potatoes are the pick of the crop.*

picture of something the perfect example of something; an exact image of something. □ *The young newlyweds were the picture of* happiness. □ *My doctor told me that I was the picture of good health.*

piece of cake something very easy to do. □ *Winning the game was a piece of cake.* □ *Can I do it? Sure I can. Piece of cake.*

piercing scream a very loud and shrill scream. □ *Suddenly, there was a piercing scream from the next room.* □ *Bob heard Susan's piercing scream and ran to help her.*

pillar of strength AND **pillar of support** someone or something that provides support as a pillar does. □ *My parents are my pillars of support.* □ *The religious woman looked to God as her pillar of strength.*

pillar of support See pillar of strength.

piping hot [of food] extremely hot. □ *On a cold day, I like to eat piping hot soup.* □ *Be careful! This coffee is piping hot!*

pique someone's curiosity AND **pique someone's interest** to arouse interest; to arouse curiosity. □ *The advertisement piqued my curiosity about the product.* □ *The professor tried to pique the students' interest in French literature.*

pique someone's interest See pique someone's curiosity.

pitch black very black; as black as pitch. □ *The hearse was pitch black.* □ *The bandit rode on a pitch black horse and wore black clothing.*

pitch camp to set up or arrange a campsite. □ *We pitched camp near the stream.* □ *Two campers went ahead of us to pitch camp while it was still light.*

pitch one's tent to erect one's tent at a campsite. □ *The campers pitched their tents in a clearing in the woods.* □ *I pitched my tent next to a large oak tree.*

place an order to submit an order. □ *My secretary placed an order for a new computer.* □ *I placed my order only yesterday.*

place of business a place where business is done; a factory or office. □ *Our place of business opens at 9:00 A.M. each day.* □ *You will have to come to our place of business to make a purchase.*

plain English very direct and clear language; English that anyone can understand. □ *I told him what he was to do in plain English.*

☐ *That was too complicated. Please tell me again, this time in plain English.*

play a joke on someone AND **play a trick on someone** to perform a prank that deceives someone; to do something that tricks someone as a way of joking. ☐ *The children played a joke on their teacher.* ☐ *Somebody played a trick on me by hiding my shoes.*

play a trick on someone See play a joke on someone.

play ignorant to pretend to be ignorant [of something]. ☐ *I played ignorant, even though I knew about the surprise party.* ☐ *John played ignorant when I asked him if he knew who had been on the telephone.*

play innocent to pretend to be innocent and not concerned. ☐ *There is no need to play innocent. I know you broke the lamp!* ☐ *John is playing innocent, and he knows more than he is telling us.*

play one's cards close to one's vest [for someone] to work or negotiate in a careful and private manner. (Refers to holding one's playing cards close so that no one else can possibly see what one is holding.) ☐ *It's hard to figure out what John is up to because he plays his cards close to his vest.* ☐ *Don't let them know what you're up to. Play your cards close to your vest.*

plenty of something lots of something; an abundance of something; enough of something. ☐ *I have plenty of candy. Do you want some?* ☐ *This project is giving me plenty of trouble.*

plow through something to work through something with determination. ☐ *She plowed through the book to learn everything she could.* ☐ *Billy plowed through dinner and ran outside to play.*

point of view a way of thinking about something; [someone's] viewpoint; an attitude or expression of self-interest. ☐ *From my point of view, all this talk is a waste of time.* ☐ *I can understand her point of view. She has made some good observations about the problem.*

poke a hole in something AND **poke a hole through something** to make a hole in something by pushing something else through it. ☐ *The carpenter poked a hole in the wall with a nail.* ☐ *The fisherman poked a hole through the ice with a pick.*

poke a hole through something See poke a hole in something.

poles apart very different; far from coming to an agreement. (These *poles* are the extreme points, like the North Pole and the South Pole of the earth.) □ *Mr. and Mrs. Jones don't get along well. They are poles apart.* □ *They'll never sign the contract because they are poles apart.*

pose a question to ask a question; to imply the need for asking a question. □ *Genetic research poses many ethical questions.* □ *My interviewer posed a hypothetical question.*

pose as someone to pretend to be someone. □ *The impostor posed as the president of the company.* □ *My twin posed as me while I went on vacation.*

pouring rain very heavy rain. □ *The children's clothes were soaked after they played out in the pouring rain.* □ *I waited in the pouring rain for the next bus.*

the **powers that be** the people who are in authority. □ *The powers that be have decided to send back the immigrants.* □ *I have applied for a license, and the powers that be are considering my application.*

prelude to something an act or event that comes before and signals another act or event. □ *Her rudeness to her boss was a prelude to her resignation.* □ *The invasion of Poland was a prelude to World War II.*

press one's luck to expect continued good fortune; to expect to continue to escape bad luck. □ *You're okay so far, but don't press your luck.* □ *Bob pressed his luck too much and got into a lot of trouble.*

Pretty is as pretty does. You should do pleasant things if you wish to be considered pleasant. (A cliché.) □ *Now, Sally. Let's be nice. Pretty is as pretty does.* □ *My great-aunt always used to say "pretty is as pretty does" to my sister.*

pride oneself on something to feel one's pride about something one does or is. □ *The worker prided himself on his ability to do a good job.* □ *The athlete prided herself on winning all the races she entered.*

privy to something uniquely knowledgeable about something. □ *The reporter became privy to the senator's evil plan.* □ *Why are you privy to this secret information?*

prone to something likely to [do] something; apt to have something. □ *My boss is prone to fits of anger when my work isn't done.* □ *My sister is prone to sneezing because of her allergies.*

propose a toast to make a toast before drinking. □ *I'd like to propose a toast in honor of your birthday.* □ *At the wedding reception, the bride's father proposed a toast.*

prove to be something to be shown to be someone or something; to be found to be someone or something. □ *Susan proved to be a good friend when she lent me some money.* □ *The food proved to be spoiled when I smelled it.*

provided that . . . on the condition that . . . □ *I will come to your party, provided that I am invited.* □ *I will help you, provided that you pay me.*

pull a gun (on someone) AND **pull a knife (on someone)** to bring out a gun or knife so that it is ready for use against someone. □ *I screamed when the mugger pulled a knife on me.* □ *The police shot the thief when he pulled a gun.*

pull a knife (on someone) See pull a gun (on someone).

punch a hole in something to make a hole in something with something else. (See also poke a hole in something.) □ *John punched a hole in the wall with his fist.* □ *Mary punched a hole in the paper with her pencil.*

put a bee in someone's bonnet See under have a bee in one's bonnet.

put a cap on something to put a limit on something □ *We need to put a cap on spending in every department.* □ *The city put a cap on the amount each landlord could charge.*

put a hold on something place a restriction on something showing that it is reserved, delayed, or inactivated. □ *The bank put a hold on my credit card until I paid my bill.* □ *The committee agreed to put a hold on the troublesome piece of business.*

put an end to something AND **put a stop to something** to make something end; to terminate something; to stop something. □ *The teacher put an end to the fighting between the boys.* □ *Why can't the police put a stop to crime?*

put a spin on something to twist a report or story to one's advantage; to interpret an event to make it seem favorable or beneficial to oneself. □ *The mayor tried to put a positive spin on the damaging polls.* □ *The pundit's spin on the new legislation was highly critical.*

put a stop to something See put an end to something.

put in one's oar See put one's oar in.

put one's mind to something to give one's complete attention to something. □ *I could finish this job tonight if I put my mind to it.* □ *Please put your mind to it and concentrate on getting it finished.*

put one's oar in AND **put in one's oar** to give help; to interfere by giving advice; to add one's assistance to the general effort. □ *You don't need to put your oar in. I don't need your advice.* □ *I'm sorry. I shouldn't have put in my oar.*

put one's shoulder to the wheel to get busy. (Not literal.) □ *You won't accomplish anything unless you put your shoulder to the wheel.* □ *I put my shoulder to the wheel and finished the job quickly.*

put someone off to avoid responding to someone; to delay a response to someone. □ *I keep asking her, but she just keeps putting me off.* □ *Don't put me off again. Answer me now!*

put someone on to tease or kid someone; to deceive someone playfully. □ *I don't believe you! You're just putting me on!* □ *He thought you were serious, but you were just putting him on.*

put someone or something to the test to see what someone or something can achieve. □ *I think I can jump that far, but no one has ever put me to the test.* □ *I'm going to put my car to the test right now, and see how fast it will go.*

put someone to bed AND **send someone to bed** to make someone go to bed. □ *Mother put Jimmy to bed and kissed him.* □ *Sally was naughty and was sent to bed.*

put some teeth into something to increase the power of something. □ *The mayor tried to put some teeth into the new law.* □ *The statement is too weak. Put some teeth into it.*

put something off to postpone something; to schedule something for a later time. □ *I have to put off our meeting until a later time.* □ *I put off a visit to the dentist as long as I could.*

put something on to place clothing on one's body; to get into a piece of clothing. ⊺ *I put on a heavy coat to go outside in the cold.* □ *Please put this sweater on and see if it fits.*

put something to bed to complete work on something and send it on to the next step in production, especially in publishing. □ *This edition is finished. Let's put it to bed.* □ *Finish the editing of this book and put it to bed.*

put something to (good) use to apply a skill or ability; to use a skill or ability. □ *The lawyer put her training to good use for the charity.* □ *The pianist put his talents to use at the party.*

putty in someone's hands [for someone] easily influenced by someone else; excessively willing to do what someone else wishes. □ *Bob's wife is putty in his hands. She never thinks for herself.* □ *Jane is putty in her mother's hands. She always does exactly what her mother says.*

put up with someone or something to tolerate or endure someone or something; to be able to stand someone or something. □ *I cannot put up with your constant whining any longer!* □ *We can put up with John's living here until he finds a place of his own.*

quake in one's boots to be afraid; to shake from fear. □ *I was quaking in my boots because I had to go see the manager.* □ *Stop quaking in your boots, Bob. I'm not going to fire you.*

quite a few a fairly large number; more than expected. □ *Dave has quite a few problems with his car in cold weather.* □ *There are quite a few people waiting to see you.*

quote a price to name or state the charge for doing or supplying something. □ *The mechanic quoted a price of $100 to repair my car.* □ *The carpenter quoted a price for fixing up the stairs.*

racked with pain suffering from severe pain. □ *My body was racked with pain, and I nearly passed out.* □ *My head was racked with pain.*

rail at someone (about something) to complain loudly or violently to someone about something. □ *Jane railed at the treasurer about not having received her check.* □ *I am not responsible for your problems. Don't rail at me!*

raining cats and dogs raining very hard. (A cliché. Not literal, of course.) □ *It's raining cats and dogs. Look at it pour!* □ *I'm not going out in that storm. It's raining cats and dogs.*

rant (at someone) about someone or something to talk (to someone) in a loud, violent way about someone or something. □ *Anne ranted about the bad service she had received at the store.* □ *On the bus, someone was ranting at me about the end of the world.*

rap with someone to talk; to chat. □ *I rapped with the school counselor for half an hour.* □ *My neighbor rapped with me on my back porch all night.*

ravished with delight very happy or delighted; filled with happiness or delight. □ *Mary was ravished with delight when she saw the dozen roses.* □ *My parents were ravished with delight when I graduated from college.*

reach a compromise to achieve a compromise; to make a compromise. □ *After many hours of discussion, we finally reached a compromise.* □ *We were unable to reach a compromise and quit trying.*

reach an agreement to achieve an agreement; to make an agreement. □ *We reached an agreement and signed a contract.* □ *We could not reach an agreement, so we stopped negotiating.*

reach an impasse to progress to a point at which a barrier stops further progress. □ *When negotiations with management reached an impasse, the union went on strike.* □ *The discussion reached an impasse and no one was able to propose a compromise.*

the **real thing** something that is genuine and not an imitation. □ *I don't want frozen yogurt, I want the real thing! Yes, ice cream!* □ *This looks like wood, but it is really plastic. I'd rather buy the real thing.*

recognize one for what one is See recognize something for what it is.

recognize something for what it is AND **recognize one for what one is** to see and understand exactly what someone or something is or represents. □ *The disease represented a serious threat to all peoples, and Dr. Smith recognized it for what it was.* □ *I recognize you for what you are, you scoundrel!*

reconcile oneself to something to grow comfortable with an undesirable or challenging situation. □ *John reconciled himself to living alone.* □ *Anne reconciled herself to having to wear glasses.*

reduced to something brought into a certain condition or state. □ *The grieving family was reduced to tears.* □ *The poor man was reduced to begging for food.*

regardless of something without considering something; at any rate; whatever is done; whatever option is chosen. □ *Regardless of what you say, I'm still going to the club tonight.* □ *I still have to pay the telephone bill, regardless of the fact that I didn't make all those calls.*

reliance on someone or something trust and dependence on someone or something. □ *John's reliance on his family is holding him back.* □ *Reliance on sleeping pills is dangerous.*

relieve one of one's duties to fire someone. (Often used in the passive voice.) □ *I am afraid I must relieve you of your duties.* □ *After the scandal, she was relieved of her duties at the embassy.*

religious about doing something strict about something; conscientious about something. □ *Bob is religious about paying his bills on time.* □ *Max tries to be religious about practicing the piano every day.*

reluctant to do something unwilling to do something; not wanting to do something. □ *David was reluctant to admit his mistakes.* □ *The witness was reluctant to appear in court.*

remain in touch (with someone or something) See keep in touch (with someone or something).

Remember me to someone. Please carry my good wishes to someone. (The *someone* can be a person's name or a pronoun.) □ *TOM: My brother says hello. BILL: Oh, good. Please remember me to him. TOM: I will.* □ *FRED: Bye. JOHN: Good-bye, Fred. Remember me to your Uncle Tom.*

reminiscent of someone or something reminding someone about someone or something; seeming like or suggesting someone or something. □ *This fragrance is reminiscent of fresh flowers.* □ *Jane's dress is reminiscent of the style worn in the 1920s.*

reputed to thought to do, be, or have someone or something. □ *My boss is reputed to have cancer.* □ *My neighbor was reputed to have been a spy during the war.*

responsible party the person or organization responsible or liable for something. □ *I intend to find the responsible party and get some answers to my questions.* □ *Mary sued the responsible party in the car crash.*

rest in peace to lie dead peacefully for eternity. □ *We prayed that the deceased would rest in peace.* □ *The bodies of the soldiers will rest in peace.*

The **rest is history.** Everyone knows the rest of the story that I am telling. □ *BILL: Then they arrested all the officers of the corporation, and the rest is history. SUE: Can't trust anybody these days.* □ *BOB: Hey, what happened between you and Sue? BILL: We finally realized that we could never get along, and the rest is history.*

rich in something having valuable resources, characteristics, traditions, or history. □ *The entire region is rich in historical churches.* □ *Our soil is rich in important nutrients.*

right at exactly or precisely at a specific place or time. □ *Meet me here right at noon—not a minute later!* □ *The restaurant is right at the corner of First Avenue and Main Street.*

right on time right at or just before the right time; soon enough [for something or to do something]. □ *I usually arrive right on time.* □ *Is the train right on time, or will it be late?*

ring a bell to remind someone of something; to stir something in someone's memory. □ *Your name rings a bell, but I don't recognize your face.* □ *Does the phrase "under the weather" ring a bell? Do you know what it means?*

ripple of excitement a series of quiet but excited murmurs. □ *A ripple of excitement spread through the crowd.* □ *As the president came near, a ripple of excitement indicated that people could really see him.*

ripple of protest a few quiet remarks protesting something; a small amount of subdued protest. □ *There was only a ripple of protest about the new tax law.* □ *The rude comedian hardly drew a ripple of protest.*

rise and shine to get out of bed and be lively and energetic. □ *Come on children! Rise and shine! We're going to the beach.* □ *Father always calls out "Rise and shine!" in the morning when we want to go on sleeping.*

rivet someone's attention to keep someone's attention fixed [on something]. □ *The movie riveted the audience's attention.* □ *Professor Jones's lecture riveted the students' attention.*

roll out the red carpet (for someone) to put on a great show of honor and respect for a visitor. □ *The red carpet was rolled out for the foreign dignitary.* □ *The city rolled out the red carpet for the visiting queen.*

Rome wasn't built in a day. Important things don't happen overnight. (A cliché.) □ *Don't expect a lot to happen right away. Rome wasn't built in a day, you know.* □ *Don't be anxious about how fast you are growing. Rome wasn't built in a day.*

rooted in something based on something; connected to a source or cause. □ *The civil war was rooted in old ethnic hatred.* □ *This fictional book was rooted in actual events.*

round down to See round off to.

round off to AND **round up to; round down to** to express a number in the nearest whole amount or nearest group of 1, 10, 100, 1,000, $\frac{1}{10}$, $\frac{1}{100}$, $\frac{1}{1,000}$, etc. □ *When doing taxes, Anne rounded her* *figures off to the nearest dollar.* □ *These census figures are rounded up to the nearest million.*

round up to See round off to.

rub someone the wrong way to irritate someone. □ *I'm sorry I rubbed you the wrong way. I didn't mean to upset you.* □ *Don't rub her the wrong way!*

ruffle its feathers [for a bird] to point its feathers outward. □ *The bird ruffled its feathers when it was annoyed.* □ *My parrot ruffles its feathers whenever it is ready to preen itself.*

the **ruin of someone or something** the cause of destruction; a failure. □ *Your bad judgment will be the ruin of this company!* □ *The greedy politicians were the ruin of the old empire.*

rump session a meeting held after a larger meeting. □ *A rump session continued after the meeting was adjourned.* □ *A lot of business was conducted in the rump session.*

run across someone or something See come across someone or something.

run an errand to perform an errand. □ *I have to run an errand and I will be back soon.* □ *Will you run an errand for me?*

Run it by me again. See Run that by me again.

run low (on something) to near the end of a supply of something. □ *We are running low on salt. It's time to buy more.* □ *The car is running low on gas.*

running high in a state of excitement or anger. □ *Feelings were running high as the general election approached.* □ *The mood of the crowd was running high when people saw the mother slap her child.*

run of something a continuous series of events. □ *The gambler had a run of bad luck at the roulette wheel.* □ *We had a run of very hot weather last July.*

run out of patience to become annoyed after being patient for a while. □ *I finally ran out of patience and lost my temper.* □ *The boss ran out of patience with me and sent me back to my desk.*

run out of something to use up all of something and have no more. □ *We ran out of milk, so we will have to buy some more.* □ *I usually run out of money at the end of the month.*

run rampant to run, develop, or grow out of control. □ *The children ran rampant through the house.* □ *Weeds have run rampant around the abandoned house.*

run short (of something) to begin to run out of something. □ *We are running short of eggs.* □ *I always keep enough so I will never run short.*

Run that by me again. AND **Run it by me again.** Please repeat what you just said.; Please go over that one more time. (Slang.) □ *ALICE: Do you understand? SUE: No. I really didn't understand what you said. Run that by me again, if you don't mind.* □ *JOHN: Put this piece into the longer slot and the remaining piece into the slot on the bottom. SUE: Run that by me again. I got lost just after "put."* □ *MARY: Keep to the right, past the fork in the road, then turn right at the crossroads. Do you follow? JANE: No. Run it by me again.*

rush on something a large demand for something. □ *There was a rush on bottled water during the drought.* □ *During the hot summer, there was a rush on air conditioners.*

S

sage advice very good and wise advice. □ *My parents gave me some sage advice when I turned 18.* □ *I asked my uncle for some of his sage advice.*

the **same as someone or something** identical to someone or something. □ *Can you build me a birdhouse the same as yours?* □ *Have you noticed that Mary looks the same as her mother?*

sands of time the accumulated tiny amounts of time; time represented by the sand in an hourglass. □ *The sands of time will make you grow old like everyone else.* □ *My only enemy is the sands of time.*

Say cheese! an expression used by photographers to get people to smile, which they must do while saying the word *cheese*. □ *"All of you please stand still and say cheese!" said the photographer.* □ *"Is everybody ready? Say cheese!" said Mary, holding the camera to her eye.*

scale something down AND **scale something up** to make something smaller or larger by a certain amount. □ *I scaled down the guest list because I couldn't invite so many people.* □ *Scale this drawing up a bit so we can see the details.*

scale something up See scale something down.

school of thought a particular philosophy or way of thinking about something. □ *One school of thought holds that cats cause allergic reactions.* □ *I come from the school of thought that believes people should always be polite.*

scout around for someone or something to search here and there for someone or something. □ *Tom is scouting around for a date for Friday night.* □ *Please scout around for some ideas on what to cook for dinner.*

scrape something together AND **scrape something up** to find and collect something; to locate and assemble a group of things. □ *Mary scraped a few dollars together for some new books.* ⊤ *John barely scraped up enough money to pay his rent.*

scrape something up See scrape something together.

scream bloody murder AND **cry bloody murder** to scream as if something very serious has happened. (To scream as if one had found the result of a bloody act of murder.) □ *Now that Bill is really hurt, he's screaming bloody murder.* □ *There is no point in crying bloody murder about the bill if you aren't going to pay it.*

Search me. I do not know.; You can search my clothing and my person, but you won't find the answer to your question anywhere near me. (Colloquial and not too polite. The two words have equal stress.) □ *JANE: What time does Mary's flight get in? SALLY: Search me.* □ *JOHN: What kind of paint should I use on this fence? BILL: Search me.*

search something with a fine-tooth comb See go over something with a fine-tooth comb.

security against something something that keeps someone or something safe from something; protection from something. □ *Insurance provides security against theft, loss, or damage.* □ *A good education is security against unemployment.*

seeing things imagining that one sees someone or something that is not there. □ *Lisa says that she saw a ghost, but she was just seeing things.* □ *I thought I was seeing things when Bill walked into the room. Someone had told me he was out of the country.*

seek professional help to get psychiatric treatment. □ *If you are often very depressed, you should seek professional help.* □ *His friends suggested that he seek professional help.*

see someone or something as something to consider some person or thing to be a certain way or to be a certain thing; to deem someone or something to be something. □ *Bill sees the difficult project as an opportunity to learn new skills, but I just find it exhausting.* □ *John saw the new salesman as a threat to his territory.*

see someone to some place to escort someone to a place; to make sure that someone gets someplace safely; to accompany someone to a place. □ *I saw Mary to her door, and then I got back in my car and left.* □ *Bill saw his cousin to the train station, and then they parted.*

see the last of someone or something to have the final sight of or contact with someone or something. □ *I will be back to bother you again. You haven't seen the last of me!* □ *I'll be glad when I've seen the last of these mosquitoes.*

see (to it) that something is done to make sure that something is done; to make certain of something; to make certain that something happens. □ *The manager saw to it that everyone began working on time.* □ *The mayor should see that the potholes are repaired.*

send someone into some state to cause someone to be in a certain state or condition. □ *The horrifying news sent our family into hysterics.* □ *The clerk's rude behavior sent the customer into a fit of anger.*

send someone off to participate in saying good-bye to someone who is leaving. □ *We had a party to send Tom off on his vacation.* □ *Bob's parents sent him off from the airport.*

send someone to bed See put someone to bed.

serve time to spend a certain amount of time in jail. □ *The criminal served ten years in jail.* □ *After the felon served his time, he was released from prison.*

set a trap to adjust and prepare a trap to catch an animal. □ *Bill set a mousetrap and baited it with cheese.* □ *The old man set a trap to catch an annoying squirrel.*

set fire to something to light something on fire; to ignite something, often by accident. □ *The candle set fire to the curtains.* □ *I was afraid that the sparks from the fireplace would set fire to the house.*

set sail (for somewhere) to begin a trip on a ship or boat. □ *The crew set sail at sunrise.* □ *After the sailors loaded the cargo, they set sail for Europe.*

set someone or something free to release someone or something; to allow someone or something to leave, go away, depart, escape. □ *Jimmy went outside and set his balloon free.* □ *The army set the political prisoners free.*

set something to music to incorporate words into a piece of music; to write a piece of music to incorporate a set of words. □ *The musician set my lyrics to music.* □ *The rock band set the poem to music.*

set the table to arrange a table with plates and eating utensils in preparation for a meal. □ *Please help me get ready for dinner by setting the table.* □ *I set the table for six people, but only five dinner guests came.*

settle (something) (out of court) to reach an agreement without having to go through a court of law. □ *The plaintiff and defendant decided to settle before the trial.* □ *Mary and Sue settled out of court before the trial.*

set type to arrange type for printing, now usually on a computer. □ *Have you finished setting the type for page one yet?* □ *John sets type for a living.*

sever ties with someone to end a relationship or agreement suddenly and completely. □ *The company severed ties with the embezzling employee by canceling her contract.* □ *John has severed all ties with his parents.*

a **shadow of itself** See shadow of oneself.

a **shadow of oneself** AND a **shadow of itself** [someone or something that is] not as strong, healthy, full, or lively as before. (Normally with *old* or *former*, as in the examples.) □ *The sick man was a shadow of his former self.* □ *The redecorated house was merely a shadow of its old self.*

shake hands AND **shake someone's hand** to grasp someone's hand in greeting or agreement. □ *David shook my hand when he greeted me.* □ *Anne and John shook hands before their business appointment.*

Shake it (up)! Hurry up!; Move faster!; Run faster! □ *FRED: Move it, Tom! Shake it up! TOM: I can't go any faster!* □ *JANE: Move, you guys. Shake it! BILL: Hey, I'm doing the best I can!*

shake someone's hand See shake hands.

Shame on you! a phrase scolding someone for being naughty. (Typically said to a child or to an adult for a childish infraction.) □ *JOHN: I think I broke one of your figurines. MARY: Shame on* *you! JOHN: I'll replace it, of course. MARY: Thanks, I sort of liked it.* □ *"Shame on you!" said Alice. "You should have known better!"*

shed some light on something to provide some knowledge or insight about something. □ *Can anyone shed some light on this problem?* □ *Max told us that he could shed some light on the mystery.*

shoot for something to try to do something; to attempt to do something; to aim toward a goal. □ *The industrious student shot for success.* □ *The worker shot for a $2-per-hour raise.*

short for something [of a form] being a shortened form of a word or phrase. □ Photo *is short for* photograph. □ Dave *is short for* David.

a **shot in the dark** a wild guess; an uninformed guess. □ *When I answered "seven," it was just a shot in the dark.* □ *He did not make a careful estimate. It was just a shot in the dark.*

show off to do things in a way that is meant to attract attention. □ *Please stop showing off! You embarrass me.* □ *John is always showing off to his girlfriend.*

a **show of hands** a vote expressed by people raising their hands. □ *We were asked to vote for the candidates for captain by a show of hands.* □ *Bob wanted us to vote on paper, not by a show of hands, so that we could have a secret ballot.*

show one to one's seat See show someone to a seat.

show someone to a seat AND **show one to one's seat** to lead or direct someone to a place to sit. □ *May I show you to your seat, sir?* □ *The ushers showed us to our seats politely and efficiently.*

show something off to put someone or something on display. ⊤ *Mary went to the party only to show off her new hairdo.* □ *Max likes to drive around and show his new car off.*

shuttle someone or something from person to person AND **shuttle someone or something from place to place** to move or pass someone or something from person to person; to move or pass someone or something from place to place. □ *My phone call was shuttled from person to person.* □ *Mary shuttled her children from home to school to soccer practice, and then home again.*

149

shuttle someone or something from place to place See shuttle someone or something from person to person.

shy away from someone or something to avoid someone or something, especially because or as if one is shy or afraid. □ *The mail carrier shied away from the growling dog.* □ *John has shied away from snakes ever since he was bitten.*

sick (and tired) of someone or something tired of someone or something, especially something that one must do again and again or someone or something that one must deal with repeatedly. □ *I am sick and tired of cleaning up after you.* □ *Mary was sick of being stuck in traffic.*

since time immemorial since a very long time ago. □ *My hometown has had a big parade on the Fourth of July since time immemorial.* □ *Since time immemorial, the trees have blossomed each spring.*

sit around (somewhere) to sit somewhere and relax or do nothing; to sit idly somewhere. □ *Tom likes to sit around the house in shorts and a T-shirt on hot days.* □ *Too many people are just sitting around doing nothing at my office.*

sit idly by AND **stand idly by** to remain close, doing nothing to help. □ *I do not intend to stand idly by while my children need my help.* □ *The wealthy man sat idly by while the poor people starved.*

Skin me! See Give me five!

skip rope to jump over an arc of rope that is passed beneath one's feet then over one's head, repeatedly. □ *The children skipped rope on the playground.* □ *The boxer skipped rope while training.*

Slip me five! See Give me five!

Slip me some skin! See Give me five!

slower and slower at a decreasing rate of speed; slow and then even slower. □ *The car is going slower and slower and will stop soon.* □ *The dog's breathing got slower and slower as it went to sleep.*

slow going slow and difficult progress. (Compare with **going.**) □ *It was slow going at first, but I was able to finish the project by the weekend.* □ *Getting the heavy rocks out of the field is slow going.*

Smile when you say that. I will be happy to interpret that remark as a joke or as kidding. □ *JOHN: You're a real pain in the neck. BOB: Smile when you say that.* □ *SUE: I'm going to bop you on the head! JOHN: Smile when you say that!*

So far, so good. At this point in the sequence of events, everything is all right.; As things continue to progress, everything is all right. □ *The meeting is half over and everything is fine. So far, so good.* □ *Tom is doing okay in school this year. So far, so good.*

soil one's diaper(s) [for a baby] to excrete waste into its diaper. □ *The baby soiled his diapers.* □ *I detect that someone has soiled his diaper.*

sold out [of a product] completely sold with no more items remaining; [of a store] having no more of a particular product. □ *The tickets were sold out so we couldn't go to the concert.* □ *I wanted new shoes like yours, but they were sold out.*

so long as See as long as.

some creature's time has come See someone's time has come.

someone of note a person who is famous. □ *We invited a speaker of note to lecture at the next meeting.* □ *The baseball player of note was inducted into the Hall of Fame.*

Someone's not supposed to. See It's not supposed to.

someone's time has come AND **some creature's time has come** someone or some creature is about to die. □ *The poor old dog's time has come.* □ *My time has come. I'm ready to go.*

(somewhere) in the neighborhood of something approximately a particular measurement. □ *I take somewhere in the neighborhood of ten pills a day for my various ailments.* □ *My rent is in the neighborhood of $700 per month.*

sort of something somewhat; having a small amount of a characteristic; kind of. □ *I am sort of tired. Let's go home.* □ *Mary's eyes are sort of blue and sort of gray.*

sound as if . . . AND **sound like . . .** to seem, from what has been said, as if something were so; to seem, from what has been said, to be a certain way. (*Sound like* is colloquial.) □ *It sounds like you had a good vacation.* □ *You sound as if you are angry.*

sound like . . . See sound as if . . .

(So) what else is new? This isn't new. It has happened before.; Not this again. □ *MARY: Taxes are going up again. BOB: So what else is new?* □ *JOHN: Gee, my pants are getting tight. Maybe I'm putting on a little weight. SALLY: What else is new?*

spare someone something to exempt someone from having to listen to or experience something. □ *I'll spare you the details and get to the point.* □ *Please, spare me the story and tell me what you want.*

speak highly of someone or something to express a very good opinion about someone or something. □ *Tom speaks highly of the carpenter who built his deck.* □ *Bill doesn't speak very highly of the new car he just bought.*

speak ill of someone to say something bad about someone. □ *I refuse to speak ill of any of my friends.* □ *Max speaks ill of no one and refuses to repeat gossip.*

spin a yarn to tell a tale. □ *Grandpa spun an unbelievable yarn for us.* □ *My uncle is always spinning yarns about his childhood.*

square up with someone to pay someone what one owes; to pay one's share of something to someone. □ *I'll square up with you later if you pay the whole bill now.* □ *Bob said he would square up with Tom for his share of the gas.*

squeak by See just squeak by.

stand idly by See sit idly by.

stay in touch (with someone or something) See keep in touch (with someone or something).

steaming (mad) very angry; very mad; very upset. □ *The steaming coach yelled at the clumsy players.* □ *The principal was steaming mad when he found that his office had been vandalized.*

Stop the music! AND **Stop the presses!** Stop everything! (*Presses* refers to the printing presses used to print newspapers. This means that there is recent news of such magnitude that the presses must be stopped so a new edition can be printed immediately.) □ *JOHN (entering the room): Stop the music! There's a fire in the kitchen! MARY: Good grief! Let's get out of here!* □ *"Stop the presses!" shouted Jane. "I have an announcement."*

Stop the presses! See Stop the music!

stranger to something or some place someone who is new to an area or place. □ *Although John was a stranger to big cities, he enjoyed visiting New York.* □ *You are a stranger to our town, and I hope you feel welcome.*

stretch the truth to lie. □ *When he claimed to have a Ph.D., he was stretching the truth.* □ *Sally tends to stretch the truth when telling tales about her wild teenage years.*

strike a pose to position oneself in a certain posture. □ *Bob struck a pose in front of the mirror to see how much he had grown.* □ *Lisa walked into the room and struck a pose, hoping she would be noticed.*

strike home See hit home.

strike someone as something [for a thought or behavior] to affect someone in a certain way. □ *John's rude behavior struck me as odd.* □ *Mary's attitude struck me as childish.*

(stuck) in a rut kept in an established way of living that never changes. □ *David felt like he was stuck in a rut, so he went back to school.* □ *Anne was tired of being in a rut, so she moved to Los Angeles.*

Stuff a sock in it! Stop talking! (Literally, stuff a sock in your mouth to stop the noise.) □ *TOM: Hey, Henry! Can you hear me? HENRY: Be quiet, Tom. Stuff a sock in it!* □ *FRED: Hey, you still here? I want to tell you a few things! JOHN: Oh, stuff a sock in it! You're a pain.*

subject to something 1. likely to have something, such as a physical disorder. □ *The sick man was subject to dizzy spells.* □ *I am subject to frequent headaches.* **2.** tentative, depending on something; vulnerable to something. □ *I have made all the necessary plans, subject to your approval, of course.* □ *My remarks are, of course, subject to your criticisms.*

succumb to something to die of something. □ *After battling lung cancer for almost a year, Mike finally succumbed to it.* □ *In the end, she succumbed to pneumonia.*

suggestive of something reminiscent of something; seeming to suggest something. □ *Bill's homemade soup is suggestive of his mother's.* □ *The new movie was suggestive of an old one I had seen on TV.*

suit oneself to do what one wishes. □ *We don't mind whether you stay or not. Suit yourself!* □ *The boss preferred me to work late, but he told me to suit myself.*

supposed to do something expected or intended to do something; obliged or allowed to do something. □ *You're supposed to say "excuse me" when you burp.* □ *Mom says you're supposed to come inside for dinner now.*

susceptible to something 1. easily persuaded; easily influenced. □ *The students were susceptible to the allure of drugs.* □ *The young revolutionaries were susceptible to propaganda.* **2.** likely to contract a sickness; likely to become sick. □ *People with AIDS are susceptible to pneumonia.* □ *Infants and the elderly are more susceptible to illness than most other people are.*

the **sweat of one's brow** one's efforts; one's hard work. □ *Tom raised these vegetables with the sweat of his brow.* □ *Sally polished the car by the sweat of her brow.*

sweep out of some place to move or leave in a flamboyant or theatrical way. □ *The insulted customer swept out of the store.* □ *The celebrity rose from his table and swept out of the restaurant.*

table a motion to postpone the discussion of something during a meeting. □ *Mary suggested that they should table the motion.* □ *The motion for a new policy was tabled until the next meeting.*

take a bath See take a shower.

take a chance to take a gamble or a risk. □ *Max took a chance and bet on the aging horse.* □ *Don't take a chance. Look before you cross the street.*

take a course (in something) to enroll in a course and do the required work. □ *I decided to take a course in history.* □ *Bob drives into the city where he is taking a course.*

take advantage of someone to use someone unfairly for one's own advantage. □ *You took advantage of Tom by bringing a stranger to his party. He could hardly refuse to let her in!* □ *The government's complicated tax rules take advantage of the people who don't understand them.*

take advantage of something to make good use of something; to benefit from something; to benefit from an opportunity. □ *I took advantage of Max's offer of free tickets to the opera.* □ *Mary always takes advantage of every opportunity that comes her way.*

take a fancy to someone or something to develop a liking for someone or something. □ *I think that Tom has taken a fancy to Mary.* □ *Bill took a fancy to skydiving and now he does it every weekend.*

take a hike 1. to go on a hike; to go hiking. □ *It's a beautiful day. Let's take a hike in the woods.* □ *We took a hike through the forest to visit John's cabin.* **2.** to go away (and stop bothering someone). (Usually **Take a hike!**) □ *You are being annoying! Take a hike!* □ *She was bothering me, so I told her to take a hike.*

take a look at someone or something AND **have a look at someone or something** to observe or examine someone or something. □ *I asked the doctor to take a look at my cut.* □ *Would you please have another look at your work? It is not complete.*

take a look for someone or something AND **have a look for someone or something** to make a visual search for someone or something; to look for someone or something. □ *Please go to the library and have a look for a book about snakes.* □ *Take a look for a man in a black suit. He is your guide.*

take a nap to have a brief period of sleep. □ *I took a short nap just after lunch.* □ *The baby takes a long nap each afternoon.*

take an oath to swear to something; to make a vow. □ *You must take an oath that you will never tell anyone about this.* □ *When I was a witness in court, I had to take an oath that I would tell the truth.*

take a peep See have a peep.

take a potshot at someone or something to criticize someone or something; to include a criticism of someone or something in a broader or more general criticism. (Also plural, with *potshots*.) □ *Throughout the campaign, the media took potshots at the foolish politician.* □ *John was taking a potshot at me when he condemned all office workers.*

take a risk to enter a situation where there is risk; to expose oneself to risk. □ *I took a risk by standing too close to the edge of the cliff.* □ *I would never take a risk by buying stock on the stock market.*

take a shot at something See give something a shot.

take a shower AND **take a bath** to bathe. □ *I take a shower every morning.* □ *John takes a hot bath to relax.*

take a stab at something See have a stab at something.

take a toll the damage or wear that is caused by using something or by hard living. □ *Years of sunbathing took a toll on Mary's skin.* □ *Drug abuse takes a heavy toll on the lives of people.*

take attendance to make a record of persons attending something. □ *The teacher took attendance before starting the class.* □ *I will take attendance each day.*

take a vacation to go somewhere for a vacation; to stop work to have a vacation. □ *Sue took a vacation at the Grand Canyon last year.* □ *I need to take a vacation and relax.*

take care of someone or something 1. to deal with someone or something; to handle or manage someone or something. □ *Would you please take care of this little problem?* □ *This is an easy thing to take care of. I will fix it immediately.* **2.** to provide care for someone or something. □ *John and Mary took care of their aged grandmother.* □ *Please take care of my plants while I am on vacation.*

Take care (of yourself). 1. Good-bye and keep yourself healthy. □ *JOHN: I'll see you next month. Good-bye. BOB: Good-bye, John. Take care of yourself.* □ *MARY: Take care. SUE: Okay. See you later.* **2.** Take care of your health and get well. □ *MARY: Don't worry. I'll get better soon. SUE: Well, take care of yourself. Bye.* □ *JANE: I'm sorry you're ill. BOB: Oh, it's nothing. JANE: Well, take care of yourself.*

take cold See catch cold.

take inventory to make an inventory list. □ *They are taking inventory in the warehouse, counting each item and writing the number on a list.* □ *The hardware store closed once a year in order to take inventory.*

take it on the chin to experience and endure a direct (literal or figurative) blow or assault. □ *The bad news was a real shock, and John took it on the chin.* □ *The worst luck comes my way, and I always end up taking it on the chin.*

take offense at someone or something to interpret someone or something as being offensive. □ *Mary took offense at Bill's ignorant statements.* □ *I hope you don't take offense at what I just said.*

take one's time to go as slow as one wants or needs to; to use as much time as is required. □ *There is no hurry. Please take your time.* □ *Bill is very careful and takes his time so he won't make any mistakes.*

take out a loan to get a loan of money, especially from a bank. □ *Mary took out a loan to buy a car.* □ *We will have to take out a loan to pay the bills this month.*

take over (something) 1. to take control (of something); to seize control (of something). □ *The large company took over several smaller ones.* □ *If the army takes over, many things will change.* □ *The dictator hoped to take over the world.* **2.** to begin doing something that someone else was doing. □ *When you get tired of washing dishes, I'll take over.* □ *Bill took over the gardening after Mary hurt her back.* □ *You have been playing the drums long enough. Let me take over.*

take part (in something) to participate in something. □ *Bill refused to take part in the game.* □ *Everyone is asked to take part in the celebration.*

take pity on someone to feel pity for someone. □ *I took pity on the hungry puppy and gave it some food.* □ *The owner of the house took pity on us and let us come in out of the rain.*

take place to happen. □ *When will the party take place?* □ *The accident took place on the highway near the airport.*

take precedence over someone or something have the right to come before someone or something else. □ *Ambulances take precedence over regular cars at intersections.* □ *My manager's concerns take precedence over mine.*

take pride in something to do something with pride; to have pride for or about something. □ *The union workers took pride in their work.* □ *The artist took pride in her paintings.*

take shape [for something, such as plans, writing, ideas, arguments, etc.] to begin to be organized and specific. □ *My plans are beginning to take shape.* □ *As my manuscript took shape, I started showing it to publishers.*

take someone by surprise to startle someone; to surprise someone with something unexpected. □ *Oh! You took me by surprise because I didn't hear you come in.* □ *Bill took his mother by surprise by coming to the door and pretending to be a solicitor.*

take someone hostage to kidnap or seize someone as a hostage. □ *The terrorists planned to take the ambassador hostage.* □ *The entire family was taken hostage by the robber.*

take someone's part to take a side in an argument; to support someone in an argument. □ *My sister took my mother's part in* *the family argument.* □ *You are always taking the part of the underdog!*

take someone's pulse to measure the frequency of the beats of a person's pulse. □ *I can take my own pulse.* □ *The nurse took my pulse and said I was fine.*

take something at face value to accept something just as it is presented. □ *John said he wanted to come to the party, and I took that at face value. I'm sure he'll arrive soon.* □ *He made us a promise, and we took his word at face value.*

take something personally to interpret a remark as if it were mean or critical about oneself. □ *Don't take it personally, but I can't eat the cake you baked because it's too sweet.* □ *I want to tell you something, but please don't take it personally.*

take the initiative to take the first action; to make the first move on an issue. □ *Anne took the initiative to discuss problems among the staff.* □ *When the ceiling started to leak, John took the initiative and fixed the roof immediately.*

take the rap (for something) to receive the blame for something. □ *One criminal took the rap for the entire gang.* □ *David took the rap for his brother's crime.*

take (the) roll See call (the) roll.

take turns (at something) See take turns (doing something).

take turns (doing something) AND **take turns (at something); take turns (with something)** [for two or more people] to alternate in doing something. □ *Bill and I take turns washing the dishes.* □ *Let's take turns with the various chores.* □ *Mary and Sue took turns at the computer until both had finished their work.*

take turns (with something) See take turns (doing something).

take umbrage at something to feel that one has been insulted by something. □ *The employee took umbrage at not getting a raise.* □ *Mary took umbrage at the suggestion that she was being unreasonable.*

the **talk of some place** someone or something that is the subject of much conversation in a certain place, especially the town. □ *The handsome new teacher was the talk of the town.* □ *John's new car is the talk of the office.*

talk someone into doing something to persuade someone to do something; to convince someone to do something. □ *Mary talked Hank into going skiing with her.* □ *I never need to talk my friends into having a party.*

a **taste of something** an experience; an example. □ *Bill gave Sue a taste of her own rudeness.* □ *My friend used a parachute and got a taste of what it's like to be a bird.*

the **teacher's pet** the teacher's favorite student. (To be treated like a pet, such as a cat or a dog.) □ *Sally is the teacher's pet. She always gets special treatment.* □ *The other students don't like the teacher's pet.*

Tell me another. Tell me another story, explanation, or excuse that is as useless as that one. □ *So, you are late to class because your dog stole your lunch. Tell me another.* □ *You couldn't finish the report because the janitor made you leave the building. Tell me another.*

terminate someone 1. to fire someone. □ *The manager terminated the troublesome employee.* □ *If your work habits do not improve, we may be forced to terminate you.* **2.** to kill someone. □ *The agent received an order to terminate Jones.* □ *If anyone should see you, terminate him at once.*

Thanks a million. Thank you a lot. □ *BILL: Oh, thanks a million. You were very helpful. BOB: Just glad I could help.* □ *JOHN: Here's your book. JANE: Thanks a million. Sorry I needed it back in such a rush.*

Thanks, but no thanks. Thank you, but I am not interested. (A way of turning down something that is not very desirable.) □ *ALICE: How would you like to buy my old car? JANE: Thanks, but no thanks.* □ *JOHN: What do you think about a trip over to see the Wilsons? SALLY: Thanks, but no thanks. We don't get along.*

That'll be the day! It will be a very surprising day when that happens. □ *You think the Cubs will win the World Series? That'll be the day!* □ *Jane made all A's in school? That'll be the day!*

That's easy for you to say. You can say that easily because it really does not affect you the way it affects others. □ *WAITER: Here's your check. MARY: Thanks. (turning to others) I'm willing to just split the check evenly. BOB: That's easy for you to say. You had lobster!* □ *SALLY: Let's each chip in ten bucks and buy him a* *sweater.* SUE: *That's easy for you to say. You've got ten bucks to spare.*

That's the last straw! That is going too far, and now something will have to be done. □ BOB: *Now they say I have to have a tutor to pass calculus.* MARY: *That's the last straw! I'm going straight up to that school and find out what they aren't doing right.* □ *"That's the last straw!" cried Fred when he got another special tax bill from the city.*

That's the ticket! That is what is required! □ MARY: *I'll just get ready and drive the letter directly to the airport!* SUE: *That's the ticket. Take it right to the airport post office.* □ BOB: *I've got it! I'll buy a new computer!* BILL: *That's the ticket!*

That takes the cake! 1. That is good, and it wins the prize! (Assuming that the prize is a cake.) □ *"What a performance!" cheered John. "That takes the cake!"* □ SUE: *Wow! That takes the cake! What a dive!* RACHEL: *She sure can dive!* **2.** That is the end!; That does it!; That surpasses everything! (Usually refers to something that is very annoying, mean, or stupid.) □ BOB: *What a dumb thing to do, Fred!* TOM: *Yeah, Fred. That takes the cake!* □ BOB: *Wow! That takes the cake!* BILL: *What is it? Why are you slowing down?* BOB: *That stupid driver ahead of me just stopped in the middle of the highway and started backing up.*

There are no flies on someone. Someone is not slow.; Someone is not wasting time. (Someone who is lively and moves very fast could not possibly be mistaken for being dead and rotting, and therefore would not attract flies.) □ *He does twice as much work as the others. There are no flies on him.* □ *No flies on Mary. She is always busy.*

There, now. See There, there.

There, there. AND **There, now.** an expression used to comfort someone. □ *There, there. You'll feel better after you take a nap.* □ *There, now. Everything will be all right.*

There you are. That's the way things are.; This is the way things have worked out. (A fatalistic dismissal. Often with *so*, as in the examples.) □ *"There's nothing more that can be done. We've done what we could. So there you are," said Fred dejectedly.* □ ANDREW: *Then what happened?* BOB: *Then they put me in a cell until they found I was innocent. Somebody stole my watch in there, and I cut*

*myself on a broken wine bottle left on a bench. And now I've got
lice. All because of mistaken identity. So, there you are.*

There you go! Now you are doing it right!; Now you have the right
attitude! □ *ALICE: I know I can do it. I just need to try harder.
JANE: There you go!* □ *BOB: I'll devote my full time to studying
and stop messing around. FATHER: There you go! That's great!*

They must have seen you coming. You were really cheated.;
They saw you coming and decided they could cheat you easily.
□ *ANDREW: It cost two hundred dollars. RACHEL: You paid two
hundred dollars for that thing? Boy, they must have seen you coming.* □ *BOB: Do you think I paid too much for this car? It's not as
good as I thought it was. TOM: It's almost a wreck. They must have
seen you coming.*

think highly of someone or something to have a very good
opinion of someone or something. □ *Mary thinks highly of her
efficient secretary.* □ *I think highly of this very useful encyclopedia.*

Think nothing of it. AND **Don't give it another thought.; Don't
give it a (second) thought. 1.** You're welcome.; It was nothing.; I was glad to do it. □ *MARY: Thank you so much for driving me home. JOHN: Think nothing of it.* □ *SUE: It was very kind
of you to bring these all the way out here. ALICE: Think nothing
of it. I was delighted to do it.* **2.** You did no harm at all. (A very
polite way of reassuring someone that an action has not caused
any great harm or hurt the speaker.) □ *SUE: Oh, sorry. I didn't
mean to bump you! BOB: Think nothing of it.* □ *JANE: I hope I
didn't hurt your feelings when I said you were too loud. BILL:
Don't give it a second thought. I was too loud.*

a **thirst for something** a craving or desire for something. □ *The
tyrant had an intense thirst for power.* □ *The actor's thirst for fame
caused him to become unscrupulous.*

thirsty for something craving or desiring something. □ *The students were thirsty for knowledge.* □ *That evil tyrant is thirsty for
power.*

This is my floor. a phrase said by someone at the back of an elevator suggesting that people make way for an exit at a particular floor. □ *Mary said, "This is my floor," and everyone made room*

for her to get out of the elevator. □ *"Out, please," said Tom loudly.* *"This is my floor!"*

This one's on me. I will pay for the treat this time. (Usually said in reference to buying drinks or food.) □ *As the waiter set down the glasses, Fred said, "This one's on me."* □ *JOHN: Check, please.* *BILL: No, this one's on me.*

thread one's way through something to make a path for one-self through some thing or place that is filled with obstacles; to make one's way through an area that is crowded with people or things. □ *The spy threaded his way through the crowd.* □ *The bicyclists threaded their way through the cars stopped in traffic.*

thread through something to travel through something or some place where there are many obstacles; to travel through an area that is crowded with people or things. □ *The spy threaded through the crowd near the palace.* □ *The joggers threaded through the shoppers on the sidewalks.*

Three cheers! We are very pleased.; That is good news. □ *The plane landed safely and on time. Three cheers!* □ *Three cheers! Our team won!*

throw a party (for someone) to have a party; to hold a party; to arrange a party. □ *Bill threw a party for his sister before she went away to college.* □ *Things seem sort of dull. Let's throw a party.*

throw one's voice to project one's voice so that it seems to be coming from some other place. □ *The ventriloquist threw his voice.* □ *Jane can throw her voice, so I thought she was standing behind me. Actually, she was on the other side of the room.*

throw something into the bargain to include something in a deal. □ *To encourage me to buy a new car, the car dealer threw a free radio into the bargain.* □ *If you purchase three pounds of chocolates, I'll throw one pound of salted nuts into the bargain.*

thumbnail sketch a short or brief synopsis or summary. □ *The manager wrote a thumbnail sketch of her plans.* □ *The student gave the teacher a thumbnail sketch of his project.*

time flies time passes very quickly. □ *I didn't really think it was so late when the party ended. Doesn't time fly?* □ *Time simply flew when the old friends got together.*

Time hangs heavy on someone's hands. Time seems to go slowly when one has nothing to do. □ *I don't like it when time hangs so heavily on my hands.* □ *John looks so bored. Time hangs heavy on his hands.*

Time is money. [My] time is valuable, so don't waste it. □ *I can't afford to spend a lot of time standing here talking. Time is money, you know!* □ *People who keep saying "Time is money" may be working too hard.*

The **time is ripe.** It is exactly the right time. □ *I'll tell her the good news when the time is ripe.* □ *Ask the question again. The time is ripe.*

time off a period of time during which one does not have to work; free time. □ *The next time I have some time off, I want to go to Miami.* □ *I don't have any time off until next week.*

time to catch one's breath enough time to relax or behave normally. □ *When things slow down around here, I'll get time to catch my breath.* □ *Sally was so busy she didn't even have time to catch her breath.*

to no avail of no benefit or help. □ *We struggled to no avail and lost the battle.* □ *We called to tell Jane the concert was canceled, but to no avail—she had already left home.*

torn between something and something else troubled by a choice or dilemma. □ *Jane was torn between two bad choices.* □ *We were torn between telling our boss the bad news and keeping it a secret.*

to someone's liking fitting someone's personal preferences. □ *I had my house painted, but the job was not to my liking.* □ *Large meals with lots of fat are not to Bob's liking.*

toss a salad to mix the greens of a salad together with dressing. □ *The chef tossed the salad.* □ *I tossed the salad just before my guests arrived.*

to the best of my knowledge See (as) far as I know.

to wit namely; that is; that is to say. □ *The criminal was punished; to wit, he received a twenty-year sentence.* □ *Several students—to wit, Mary, Bill, Sue, and Anne—complained about their teacher.*

train one's sights on something AND **have one's sights trained on something** to have something as a goal; to direct something or oneself toward a goal. □ *You should train your sights on getting a promotion in the next year.* □ *Lisa has her sights trained on a new car.*

travesty of justice a miscarriage of justice; an act of the legal system that is an insult to the perception of justice. □ *The jury's verdict was a travesty of justice.* □ *The lawyer complained that the judge's ruling was a travesty of justice.*

the **tricks of the trade** the skills and knowledge necessary to do something. (Often with *all.*) □ *Tom can repair car engines. He knows the tricks of the trade.* □ *If I knew all the tricks of the trade, I could be a better plumber.*

trick someone into doing something to fool someone; to deceive someone; to cheat someone. □ *The thief tricked John into giving him $10.* □ *Mary tricked her friends into paying for her dinner.*

Trust me! Please believe me, because what I am telling you is true. □ *Tom said with great conviction, "Trust me! I know exactly what to do!"* □ *MARY: Do you really think we can keep this party a secret until Thursday? SALLY: Trust me! I know how to plan a surprise party.*

try one's wings (out) to try to do something one has recently become qualified to do. □ *I recently learned to snorkel, and I want to go to the seaside to try my wings.* □ *You've read about it enough. It's time to try your wings out.*

turn of the century the time when the year changes to one with two final zeros, such as from 1899 to 1900. □ *My family moved to America at the turn of the century.* □ *That poet was born before the turn of the last century.*

turn out (that) to happen; to end up; to result. □ *After it was all over, it turned out that both of us were pleased with the bargain.* □ *Have you heard how the game turned out?*

turn the other cheek to ignore abuse or an insult. (Biblical.) □ *When Bob got mad at Mary and yelled at her, she just turned the other cheek.* □ *Usually I turn the other cheek when someone is rude to me.*

unaccustomed to someone or something not used to someone or something. □ *The poor family was unaccustomed to going to fancy restaurants.* □ *Bill was unaccustomed to typing his own letters.*

under a cloud (of suspicion) to be suspected of (doing) something. □ *Someone stole some money at work, and now everyone is under a cloud of suspicion.* □ *Even the manager is under a cloud.*

under construction being built or repaired. □ *We cannot travel on this road because it's under construction.* □ *Our new home has been under construction all summer. We hope to move in soon.*

under control manageable; restrained and controlled; not out of control. □ *We finally got things under control and functioning smoothly.* □ *The doctor felt that she had the disease under control and that I would get well soon.*

under normal circumstances normally; usually; typically. □ *"We'd be able to keep the dog at home under normal circumstances,"* said Mary to the vet. □ *"Under normal circumstances you'd be able to return to work in a week,"* explained the doctor.

under oath bound by an oath; having taken an oath. □ *You must tell the truth because you are under oath.* □ *I was placed under oath before I could testify in the trial.*

under scrutiny being watched or examined closely. □ *The jeweler only noticed the flaw in the diamond under close scrutiny.* □ *The suspect was kept under scrutiny throughout the investigation.*

under pressure experiencing something that causes stress or anxiety. (Often includes a general amount, such as *some, more,* or *a lot of.*) □ *I have a headache because I'm under a lot of pressure at work.* □ *The professor's children were under pressure to do well in school.*

under the counter [for something to be bought or sold] in secret or illegally. (Also used literally.) ☐ *The drugstore owner was arrested for selling liquor under the counter.* ☐ *This owner was also selling dirty books under the counter.*

under the influence affected by alcohol; drunk. ☐ *John was under the influence when he was driving and could have caused an accident.* ☐ *Never operate machinery if you are under the influence.*

under the influence of someone or something experiencing the effects of something such as alcohol or drugs, or of any controlling power or person. ☐ *I think that guy is under the influence of drugs.* ☐ *Bill has lived under the influence of his mother for too long.*

under the weather ill. ☐ *I'm feeling a little under the weather, so I won't be in today.* ☐ *I was sorry to hear you're under the weather.*

until all hours until very late. ☐ *Mary is out until all hours, night after night.* ☐ *If I'm up until all hours two nights in a row, I'm just exhausted.*

up for something enthusiastic about something. ☐ *Are you up for a hike through the woods?* ☐ *I'm really up for my job interview today.*

up in the air undecided; uncertain. ☐ *I don't know what Sally plans to do. Things were sort of up in the air the last time we talked.* ☐ *Let's leave this question up in the air until next week.*

upon impact at the place or time of an impact. ☐ *The car crumpled upon impact with the brick wall.* ☐ *The man who fell from the top of the building died on impact.*

up to doing something able to do something. ☐ *Do you feel up to going back to work today?* ☐ *She just isn't up to driving all night.*

up to one's ears (in something) See up to one's neck (in something).

up to one's neck (in something) AND **up to one's ears (in something)** very much involved in something. ☐ *I can't come to the meeting. I'm up to my neck in these reports.* ☐ *Mary is up to her ears in her work.*

up to something doing something, especially something bad or scheming. (This *something* does not vary.) ☐ *Max is up to* *something, I see.* □ *The children are being quiet, so they must be up to something.*

used to do something to have done something [customarily] in the past. (Compare with **be used to someone or something.**) □ *We used to go swimming in the lake before it became polluted.* □ *I used to eat nuts, but then I became allergic to them.*

use foul language to swear. □ *There's no need to use foul language.* □ *When she gets angry, she tends to use foul language.*

the **very last** the end; an absolute end of something. □ *At the very last of the movie, the hero gets killed.* □ *Bill stayed at the party until the very last.*

the **very thing** the exact thing that is required. □ *The vacuum cleaner is the very thing for cleaning the stairs.* □ *I have the very thing to remove that stain.*

visually impaired blind or partly blind. □ *I am visually impaired, but I like TV just as much as the next person.* □ *The disease left him visually impaired.*

vote a split ticket to cast a ballot on which the votes are divided between two or more parties. □ *I always vote a split ticket, since I detest both parties.* □ *Mary voted a split ticket for the first time in her life.*

vote a straight ticket to cast a ballot with all the votes for members of the same political party. □ *I'm not a member of any political party, so I never vote a straight ticket.* □ *I usually vote a straight ticket because I believe in the principles of one party and not in those of the other.*

walk off with something 1. to steal something. □ *Did you see that kid walk off with that candy bar?* □ *The crook just walked off with a $30 necktie.* **2.** to win something easily. □ *The other team walked off with the game.* □ *The home team walked off with the win.*

wall-to-wall with something having something in all places. □ *The hallway is wall-to-wall with Jimmy's toys.* □ *The beach was wall-to-wall with tourists.*

want for nothing not to lack anything; to have everything one needs or desires. □ *The Smiths don't have much money, but their children seem to want for nothing.* □ *Lisa's husband spoils her. She wants for nothing.*

wash one's hands of someone or something to end one's association with someone or something. □ *I washed my hands of Tom. I wanted no more to do with him.* □ *That car was a real headache. I washed my hands of it long ago.*

Watch it! 1. Be careful! □ *RACHEL: Watch it! There's a broken stair there. JANE: Gee, thanks.* □ *MARY: Watch it! There's a pothole in the street. BOB: Thanks.* **2.** Do not act or talk that way. □ *SALLY: I really hate John! SUE: Watch it! He's my brother!* □ *BILL: You girls always seem to take so long to do a simple thing like getting dressed. MARY: Watch it!*

watch one's step to act with care and caution so as not to make a mistake. □ *John had better watch his step with the new boss. She won't put up with his lateness.* □ *Mary was told by her adviser to watch her step and stop missing classes or she would be asked to leave college.*

watch over someone or something to monitor or guard someone or something □ *Please watch over my apartment while I am* *on vacation.* □ *I am looking for someone to watch over my grand-mother during the day.*

watch someone or something like a hawk to watch someone or something very carefully. □ *The teacher watched the pupils like a hawk to make sure they did not cheat on the exam.* □ *We had to watch our dog like a hawk in case he ran away.*

Watch your mouth! See Watch your tongue!

Watch your tongue! AND **Watch your mouth!** Do not talk like that!; Do not say those things!; Do not say those bad words! □ *ANDREW: Don't talk to me like that! Watch your tongue! BILL: I'll talk to you any way I want.* □ *"Watch your mouth!" warned Sue. "I will not listen to any more of this slime!"*

water under the bridge past and forgotten. (A cliché.) □ *Please don't worry about it anymore. It's all water under the bridge.* □ *I can't change the past. It's water under the bridge.*

(way) over there in a place some distance away. □ *I see a house way over there in the field.* □ *My hat is over there on the table.*

We aim to please. We try to make people happy and satisfied. (Usually heard in a shop or in a service business.) □ *I am happy to help one of our best customers. We aim to please.* □ *Thank you for making your purchase. We aim to please.*

a **wealth of something** a large amount of something. □ *There's a wealth of information on parrots at the library.* □ *The junkyard had a wealth of used car parts.*

wear and tear damage that is caused because of continued use. □ *Children's clothing must withstand a lot of wear and tear.* □ *Due to five years of wear and tear, the dishwasher broke.*

weather permitting if the weather allows it. □ *Weather permitting, we will be there on time.* □ *The plane lands at midnight, weather permitting.*

wed(ded) to someone married to someone. □ *The couple will have been wed to each other for fifty years next June.* □ *Anne is wedded to one of my cousins.*

wedded to something mentally attached to something; firmly committed to something. □ *The manager was wedded to the idea of getting new computers.* □ *The mayor was wedded to the new budget plan.*

weeks running See days running.

We just can't take you anywhere anymore. You always make a mess or embarrass yourself, so we cannot take you to a nice party, restaurant, concert, etc. (Usually jocular and teasing.) □ *Wow, Uncle Charlie, you dumped your dinner in your lap. We just can't take you anywhere anymore.* □ *John, you always say the wrong thing when you are introduced to someone. We just can't take you anywhere anymore.*

welcome to do something free to do something; allowed to do something. □ *The audience is welcome to ask questions at the end of the speech.* □ *You are welcome to help yourself to anything in the kitchen.*

well-fixed See well-heeled.

We('ll) have to do lunch sometime. AND **Let's do lunch (sometime).** We must have lunch together sometime. (A vague statement that may lead to lunch plans but often does not.) □ *RACHEL: Nice to talk to you, Tom. We have to do lunch sometime. TOM: Yes, good to see you. I'll phone you.* □ *TOM: Can't talk to you now. Catch you later. MARY: We'll have to do lunch sometime.* □ *JOHN: Good to see you, Tom. TOM: Right. Let's do lunch sometime. JOHN: Good idea. I'll call you. Bye. TOM: Right. Bye.* □ *MARY: Catch you later. SUE: Sure. Let's do lunch. MARY: Okay. Call me. Bye.*

well-heeled AND **well-fixed; well-off** wealthy; with sufficient money. □ *My uncle can afford a new car. He's well-heeled.* □ *Everyone in his family is well-off.*

well-off See well-heeled.

(Well,) what do you know! a way of expressing surprise at finding something that is unexpected; an expression of mild surprise at something someone has said. (No answer is expected or desired.) □ *ANDREW: Well, what do you know! Here's a brand new shirt in this old trunk. BOB: I wonder how it got there.* □ *TOM: These two things fit together like this. JOHN: Well, what do you know!*

What are you drinking? **1.** a phrase inquiring what someone is already drinking so that the person who asks the question can offer another drink of the same thing. □ *TOM: What are you drinking? BILL: Scotch and water. TOM: I'll get you another.*

□ WAITER: *What are you drinking, madam?* SUE: *It's just soda. No more, thanks.* WAITER: *Very good.* **2.** a phrase inquiring what is being drunk at a particular gathering, so that the person asking can request the same drink. (A way of finding out what drinks are available.) □ MARY: *Do you want a drink?* SUE: *Yes, thanks. Say, that looks good. What are you drinking?* MARY: *It's just ginger ale.* □ BILL: *Can I get you something to drink?* JANE: *What are you drinking?* BILL: *I'm having gin and tonic.* JANE: *I'll have that too, thanks.*

What brings you here? What is your reason for being here? (A polite request for this information. More polite than "Why are you here?") □ TOM: *Hello, Mary. What brings you here?* MARY: *I was invited, just like you.* □ DOCTOR: *Well, John, what brings you here?* JOHN: *I've had this cough for nearly a month, and I think it needs looking into.*

What does that prove? So what?; That does not mean anything. (A defensive expression. The heaviest stress is on *that*. Often with *so*, as in the examples.) □ TOM: *It seems that you were in the apartment the same night that it was robbed.* BOB: *So, what does that prove?* TOM: *Nothing, really. It's just something we need to keep in mind.* □ RACHEL: *You're late again on your car payment.* JANE: *What does that prove?* RACHEL: *Simply that you can't afford the car, and we are going to repossess it.*

What do you know? See Well, what do you know?

What do you know for sure? How are you?; What do you know? (Familiar. Does not require a direct answer.) □ TOM: *Hey, man! What do you know for sure?* BILL: *Howdy, Tom. What's new?* □ JOHN: *How are you doing, old buddy?* BILL: *Great, you ugly beast!* JOHN: *What do you know for sure?* BILL: *Nothing.*

What do you say? 1. Hello, how are you? (Informal.) □ BOB: *What do you say, Tom?* TOM: *Hey, man. How are you doing?* □ BILL: *What do you say, man?* FRED: *What's the good word, you old so-and-so?* **2.** What is your answer or decision? □ BILL: *I need an answer from you now. What do you say?* BOB: *Don't rush me!* □ SUE: *I can offer you $700 for your old car. What do you say?* BOB: *I'll take it!* **3.** an expression urging a child to say "thank you" or "please." □ MOTHER: *Here's a nice glass of milk.* CHILD: *Good.* MOTHER: *What do you say?* CHILD: *Very good.* MOTHER: *No.*

What do you say? CHILD: Thank you. □ *When Aunt Sally gave Billy some candy, his mother said to Billy, "What do you say?" "Thank you," said Billy.*

What else is new? See So what else is new?

What(ever) will be, will be. Whatever happens will happen, and there is nothing that any of us can do about it. □ *It looks like it will rain today and ruin the picnic. What will be, will be.* □ *I am afraid that my injured dog will die. Whatever will be, will be.*

What for? Why?; For what reason? □ *"I want you to clean your room." "What for? It's clean enough."* □ *"You must always carry some identification." "What for? Everyone here knows me."*

What gives? What is happening?; What is going on?; Explain what the problem is. (Informal.) □ *Why are you so excited? What gives?* □ *What gives? Why are all the students laughing?*

what if what would be the result if something were true? □ *What if you had all the money you want?* □ *What if everyone thought you were great?*

what makes someone tick that which motivates someone; that which makes someone behave in a certain way. □ *William is sort of strange. I don't know what makes him tick.* □ *When you get to know people, you find out what makes them tick.*

what makes something tick that which causes something to run or function. □ *I don't know what makes it tick.* □ *I took apart the radio to find out what made it tick.*

What's cooking? What is happening?; How are you? (Colloquial or slang.) □ *BOB: Hi, Fred! What's cooking? FRED: How are you doing, Bob?* □ *TOM: Hey, Bill! What's cooking? BILL: Nothing. Anything happening with you?*

What's eating someone? What is upsetting or bothering someone?; What is making someone so irritable? □ *What's eating John? He seems to be mad at all of us.* □ *What's wrong, Bob? What's eating you?*

What's in it for me? What is the benefit for me in this scheme? □ *BOB: Now that plan is just what is needed. BILL: What's in it for me? What do I get out of it?* □ *SUE: We signed the Wilson contract yesterday. MARY: That's great! What's in it for me?*

What's it to you? Why does it matter to you?; It's none of your business. (Colloquial and a bit contentious.) □ *TOM: Where are you going? JANE: What's it to you?* □ *MARY: Bill's pants don't match his shirt. JANE: Does it matter? What's it to you?*

What's keeping someone? What is delaying someone? □ *BOB: Wasn't Mary supposed to be here? BILL: I thought so. BOB: Well, what's keeping her? BILL: How should I know?* □ *BILL: I've been waiting here for an hour for Sally. SUE: What's keeping her?*

What's the (big) idea? Why did you do that?; I am shocked at what you did.; Why did you do that in such an arrogant way? □ *You pushed in line ahead of me. What's the big idea?* □ *What's the idea? You had no cause to do that.*

What's the damage? What is the amount of the bill?; What are the charges? □ *That was a very good meal. What's the damage?* □ *What's the damage? Do you accept credit cards?*

What was the name again? Please tell me your name again. (More typical of a clerk than of someone just introduced.) □ *CLERK: What was the name again? BILL: Bill.* □ *"What was the name again? I didn't write it down," confessed Fred.*

when least expected when something is not expected to happen. □ *Something will go wrong with our plans when least expected.* □ *The worst kinds of problems occur when least expected.*

When the cat's away, the mice will play. Some people will get into mischief when they are not being watched. (A cliché.) □ *The students behaved very badly for the substitute teacher. When the cat's away, the mice will play.* □ *John had a wild party at his house when his parents were out of town. When the cat's away, the mice will play.*

Where do we go from here? 1. What direction should we take from this location? □ *Well, we got as far as the main road. Where do we go from here?* □ *We seem to be lost. Where do we go from here?* **2.** What is the next thing that we should do as a part of the process or plan? □ *We have completed most of the work. Where do we go from here?* □ *Where do we go from here? There is nothing left to do.* **3.** We have used up all of our options and there seems to be nothing effective that we can do. □ *Things are in a hopeless mess. Where do we go from here?* □ *Where do we go from here? It looks like the whole plan is ruined.*

175

Where (have) you been keeping yourself? I haven't seen you for a long time. Where have you been? □ *BILL: Hi, Alice! Where've you been keeping yourself? ALICE: Oh, I've been around. How are you doing? BILL: Okay.* □ *JOHN: What's up? BILL: Hey, man. Where you been keeping yourself? JOHN: Oh, I've been busy.*

Where's the fire? Where are you going in such a hurry? (Typically said by a police officer to a driver who has just been caught speeding.) □ *OFFICER: Okay, where's the fire? MARY: Was I going a little fast?* □ *"Where's the fire?" Bob called ahead to Sue, who had gotten well ahead of him in her excitement.*

whether or not either if something is the case or if something is not the case; one way or the other. □ *I'll drive to New York tomorrow whether or not it rains.* □ *I'm going to the mall whether you come with me or not.*

wild about someone or something very excited about someone or something. □ *I'm just wild about comedies.* □ *John is wild about antique cars.*

will bear watching will need watching; deserves observation or monitoring. (This is the verb *to bear.*) □ *This problem will bear watching.* □ *This is a very serious disease, and it will bear watching for further developments.*

Will wonders never cease? This is simply amazing! □ *Look, an electric powered car! Will wonders never cease?* □ *What an amazing movie! Will wonders never cease?*

window-shopping the habit or practice of looking at goods in shop windows or stores without actually buying anything. □ *Mary and Jane do a lot of window-shopping during their lunch hour, looking for things to buy when they get paid.* □ *Alice said she was just window-shopping, but she bought a new coat.*

Wipe that smile off your face! Don't smile, because this is supposed to be very serious. □ *This is not funny. Wipe that smile off your face!* □ *Wipe that smile off your face! You are not here to have a good time!*

with all one's heart and soul very sincerely. □ *Oh, Bill, I love you with all my heart and soul, and I always will!* □ *She thanked us with all her heart and soul for the gift.*

with all the fixings with all the condiments that accompany a certain kind of food. □ *For $5.99, you get a turkey dinner with all the fixings.* □ *Max likes his hamburgers with all the fixings.*

with a vengeance with determination and eagerness. □ *The angry soldier attacked the enemy with a vengeance.* □ *Bill ate all his dinner and gobbled up his dessert with a vengeance.*

with ease without effort. □ *The smart student passed the test with ease.* □ *The gymnast did a back flip with ease.*

with impunity without risk of punishment; with immunity from the negative consequences of an act; while being exempt from punishment. □ *The diplomat parked in illegal parking spaces with impunity.* □ *Bob used his brother's property with impunity.*

with one's tail between one's legs appearing frightened or cowardly, like a frightened or defeated dog; appearing threatened or humiliated. □ *John seems to lack courage. When people criticize him unjustly, he just goes away with his tail between his legs and doesn't tell them they're wrong.* □ *The frightened dog ran away with its tail between its legs when the bigger dog growled.*

without a shadow of a doubt AND **beyond the shadow of a doubt** without the smallest amount of doubt. □ *I am certain that I am right, without a shadow of a doubt.* □ *I felt the man was guilty beyond the shadow of a doubt.*

with regard to someone or something concerning someone or something. □ *What shall we do with regard to planning dinner?* □ *With regard to Bill, I think he is working too hard.*

with relish with pleasure or enjoyment. □ *John ate his juicy orange with great relish.* □ *We sampled the excellent food with relish.*

with respect to someone or something of or about someone or something. □ *With respect to radiation, this power plant is very safe.* □ *This article examines experiments with respect to ethical issues.*

work out (somehow) to result in a good conclusion; to finish positively. □ *Don't worry. I am sure that everything will work out all right.* □ *Things always work out somehow.*

work something off to get rid of something by taking physical exercise. □ *Bob put on weight while on vacation and is trying to* *work it off by swimming regularly.* ⊤ *Jane tried to work off her depression by playing a game of tennis.*

worth one's or its weight in gold very valuable. □ *This book is worth its weight in gold.* □ *Oh, Bill. You're wonderful. You're worth your weight in gold.*

would like (to have) someone or something to want someone or something; to prefer someone or something. (*Would* is often contracted to *'d.*) □ *I would like to have three cookies.* □ *I'd like a piece of cake.* □ *Bill would like to have more friends.*

would rather would more willingly; would more readily. (*Would* is often contracted to *'d.*) □ *I would rather have an apple than a pear. I don't like pears.* □ *I'd rather live in the North than the South, because I like snow.*

wreak vengeance (up)on someone or something to seek and get revenge on someone by harming someone or something. □ *The thief wreaked his vengeance by destroying his rival's house.* □ *The general wanted to wreak vengeance on the opposing army for its recent successful attack.*

year after year for many years, one after another. □ *We go to the same place for our vacation year after year.* □ *I seem to earn the same salary year after year.*

years running See days running.

Yesterday wouldn't be too soon. an answer to the question "When do you want this?" □ *MARY: Mr. Franklin, when do you want this? FRED: Well, yesterday wouldn't be too soon.* □ *ALICE: When am I supposed to have this finished? SUE: Yesterday wouldn't be too soon.*

a **yoke around someone's neck** something that oppresses someone; a burden. □ *John's greedy children are a yoke around his neck.* □ *I bought a large house, and the huge mortgage has become a yoke around my neck.*

You ain't seen nothing yet! The best, most exciting, or cleverest part is yet to come! (The use of *ain't* is a fixed part of this idiomatic expression.) □ *ALICE: Well, the first act was simply divine. SUE: Stick around. You ain't seen nothing yet!* □ *MARY: This part of the city is really beautiful. BILL: You ain't seen nothing yet!*

You are welcome. AND **You're welcome.** a polite response to "Thank you." □ *"Thank you for helping me." "You're welcome."* □ *"Thank you very much!" "You are welcome!"*

You bet your boots! See You bet your (sweet) life!

You bet your (sweet) life! AND **You bet your boots!** You can be absolutely certain of that! (Informal and colloquial.) □ *MARY: Will I need a coat today? BILL: You bet your sweet life! It's colder than an iceberg out there.* □ *BILL: Will you be at the game Saturday? TOM: You bet your boots!*

You can say that again! That is so true or so insightful that it bears repeating. □ *BILL: Gee, it's cold today! MARY: You can say that again!* □ *BILL: This cake sure is good. FATHER: You can say that again.*

(You) can't fight city hall. There is no way to win in a battle against a bureaucracy. □ *BILL: I guess I'll go ahead and pay the tax bill. BOB: Might as well. You can't fight city hall.* □ *MARY: How did things go at your meeting with the zoning board? SALLY: I gave up. Can't fight city hall. Better things to do.*

You can't get there from here. a catchphrase said jokingly when someone asks directions to get to a place that can be reached only by a circuitous route. □ *BILL: How far is it to Adamsville? TOM: Adamsville? Oh, that's too bad. You can't get there from here.* □ *"Galesburg? Galesburg, you say?" said the farmer. "By golly, you can't get there from here!"*

You can't take it with you. You should enjoy your money now, because you won't be able to use it when you're dead. (A cliché.) □ *My uncle is a wealthy miser. I keep telling him, "You can't take it with you."* □ *If you have money, you should use it. You can't take it with you, you know!*

You could have fooled me. I would have thought otherwise.; I would have thought the opposite. □ *HENRY: Did you know that this land is among the most productive in the entire state? JANE: You could have fooled me. It looks quite barren.* □ *JOHN: I really do like Mary. ANDREW: You could have fooled me. You treat her rather badly sometimes.*

You could have knocked me over with a feather. I was extremely surprised.; I was so surprised that I was disoriented and could have been knocked over easily. □ *ANDREW: When she told me she was going to get married, you could have knocked me over with a feather. SALLY: I can see why.* □ *JOHN: Did you hear that they are going to tear down the courthouse and build a new one—price tag twelve million dollars? SALLY: Yes, and when I did, you could have knocked me over with a feather.*

You don't say. 1. a general response to something that someone has said. (Expresses a little polite surprise or interest, but not disbelief.) □ *BILL: I'm starting work on a new job next Monday. BOB: You don't say.* □ *SALLY: The Jones boys are keeping a pet snake.*

ALICE: You don't say. **2.** You have just said something that everybody already knows. □ *BILL: I think I'm beginning to put on a little weight. JANE: You don't say.* □ *JOHN: My goodness, prices are getting high. SUE: You don't say.*

You flatter yourself. You think you are better or more capable than anyone else does. □ *You think you could be president of the company? You flatter yourself.* □ *BILL: I think Mary wants to go out with me. SUE: You flatter yourself. She hasn't even noticed you.*

You got me beat. See (It) beats me.

You know what? Do you want to know what I am thinking?; I have something interesting to report. Do you want to hear about it? (Does not always require an answer.) □ *You know what? The windows are open and it's raining.* □ *You know what? Your car is smoking.*

You'll be the death of me (yet). You and your problems may, in fact, kill me. (An exaggeration, of course.) □ *HENRY: You'll be the death of me yet. Why can't you ever do anything right? ANDREW: I've got a talent for it, I guess.* □ *BILL: Mom, the teacher says you have to go to school again for a conference. MOTHER: Oh, Billy, you'll be the death of me.*

You (really) said a mouthful. You said exactly what needed to be said.; What you said was very meaningful and had great impact. (Colloquial and folksy.) □ *BILL: Did you hear what I said to her? JANE: Yes. You said a mouthful. Was she mad?* □ *BILL: This is the worst food I have ever eaten. It is either stale, wilted, dry, or soggy! TOM: You said a mouthful!*

You're asking for it! You are inviting a physical or verbal attack! □ *You're asking for it! Just keep teasing me and I will punch you.* □ *You're asking for it! I don't have to listen to your rudeness.*

You're breaking my heart. Your sad tale—which I don't believe—is causing me great grief. (Insincere and sarcastic.) □ *So, the dog ate your homework and the library didn't have the books you needed. You're breaking my heart.* □ *You're breaking my heart. What a sad tale. Next time, play some sad violin music while you tell it.*

You're the doctor. You are in a position to tell me what to do.; I yield to you and your knowledge of this matter. (The person being addressed is most likely not a physician.) □ *BILL: Eat your* *dinner, then you'll feel more like playing ball. Get some energy! TOM: Okay, you're the doctor.* □ *TEACHER: You'd better study the first two chapters more thoroughly. BOB: You're the doctor.*

You're welcome. See You are welcome.

You took the words right out of my mouth. You said exactly what I meant to say before I had a chance to say it, and, therefore, I agree with you very much. □ *BILL: I think she's old enough to know better. TOM: You took the words right out of my mouth.* □ *MARY: This movie is going to put me to sleep. JANE (yawning): You took the words right out of my mouth.*

You've got another think coming. You will have to rethink your position. (The second part of an expression something like, "If you think so-and-so, then *you've got another think coming.*" Also with *thing* rather than *think*.) □ *RACHEL: If you think I'm going to stand here and listen to your complaining all day, you've got another think coming! BILL: Frankly, I don't care what you do.* □ *ANDREW: If you think you can get away with it, you've got another think coming! BOB: Get away with what? I didn't do anything!*

You('ve) got me there. I cannot respond sensibly or accurately to what you ask or propose. □ *I am sorry but I do not know the answer. You've got me there.* □ *You've got me there. I forgot.*

Phrase-Finder Index

Use this index to find the form of a phrase that you want to look up in the dictionary. First, pick out any major word in the phrase you are seeking. Second, look the simplest form of that word up in this index to find the form of the phrase used in the dictionary. Third, look up the phrase in the main body of the dictionary.

Some of the words occurring in the dictionary entries do not appear as entries in this index. Some words are omitted because they occur so frequently that their lists would cover many pages. In these instances, you should look up the phrase under some other word. Most of the grammar or function words, such as prepositions, pronouns, and articles, are not indexed.

A everything from A to Z
abeyance in abeyance
able not able to stomach someone or something
about at sea (about something)
about Better keep quiet about it.
about Better keep still about it.
about crazy about someone or something
about feel guilty (about something)
about go into one's song and dance about something
about halfhearted (about someone or something)
about have second thoughts about someone or something
about How about a lift?
about How about that!
about I don't know about that!
about let someone know (about something)
about level with someone (about someone or something)
about mad about someone or something

about rail at someone (about something)
about rant (at someone) about someone or something
about religious about doing something
about wild about someone or something
above above par
above above reproach
absence be conspicuous by one's absence
across come across someone or something
across get something across (to someone)
across run across someone or something
act Act your age!
action course of action
activity hive of activity
add add insult to injury
advance in advance
advanced advanced in years
advantage take advantage of someone
advantage take advantage of something
advice sage advice

affinity affinity for someone or something
affirmative in the affirmative
after one thing or person after another
after year after year
again again and again
again (all) over again
again Call again.
again Here we go again.
again over again
again Run it by me again.
again Run that by me again.
again What was the name again?
again You can say that again!
against against the clock
against against the grain
against have two strikes against one
against hold a grudge (against someone)
against security against something
age Act your age!
age in this day and age
agreement in agreement
agreement reach an agreement
ahead ahead of one's time
ahead (Go ahead,) make my day!
aim We aim to please.
ain't You ain't seen nothing yet!
air air someone's dirty linen in public
air gulp for air
air nip in the air
air up in the air
alcohol under the influence (of alcohol)
all all in a day's work
all all in all
all (all) joking aside
all (all) over again
all all over but the shouting
all All right.

all All systems are go.
all all there
all all things considered
all all walks of life
all end it (all)
all first of all
all for all I know . . .
all for all the good that will do you
all Hang it all!
all I haven't got all day.
all in all my born days
all until all hours
all with all one's heart and soul
all with all the fixings
allowance make allowances for someone
allowance make allowances for something
almighty almighty dollar
am Am I glad to see you!
amends make amends (for something)
amount down by some amount
another Don't give it another thought.
another horse of another color
another one thing or person after another
another Tell me another.
another You've got another think coming.
answer answer the call
answer answer the door
any at any rate
any not going to win any beauty contests
anymore not a kid anymore
anymore We just can't take you anywhere anymore.
anyone Don't breathe a word of this to anyone.
anything Anything you say.
anything if anything happens
anything if anything should happen

barn born in a barn
bat have bats in one's belfry
bath take a bath
bathroom go to the bathroom
bay at bay
bear bear in mind that . . .
bear will bear watching
bearing have [some] bearing on something
beat beat a path to someone's door
beat beating a dead horse
beat Beat it!
beat Beats me.
beat beat the gun
beat (It) beats me.
beat (It's) got me beat.
beat You got me beat.
beauty I've got to go home and get my beauty sleep.
beauty not going to win any beauty contests
bed get out of the wrong side of the bed
bed get up on the wrong side of the bed
bed go to bed
bed put someone to bed
bed put something to bed
bed send someone to bed
bee birds and the bees
bee have a bee in one's bonnet
bee put a bee in someone's bonnet
been been had
been Been keeping cool.
been (I've) been keeping cool.
been I've been keeping myself busy.
been I've been keeping out of trouble.
been I've been up to no good.
been Where (have) you been keeping yourself?
before I've heard that one before.

before lull before the storm
beg I beg your pardon.
beg I'll have to beg off.
behalf in behalf of someone
behalf in someone's behalf
behalf on behalf of someone
behalf on someone's behalf
behind behind schedule
behind Behind you!
behold marvel to behold
belfry have bats in one's belfry
believe believe it or not
believe Believe you me!
believe Don't believe I've had the pleasure.
believe (I) don't believe I've had the pleasure.
bell ring a bell
below below average
below below par
bend bend someone's ear
bend bend the rules
benefit benefit of the doubt
bent bent on doing something
berth give someone or something a wide berth
beside beside oneself
best at its best
best at one's best
best to the best of my knowledge
bet You bet your boots!
bet You bet your (sweet) life!
better Better get on my horse.
better Better keep quiet about it.
better Better keep still about it.
better better left unsaid
better has seen better days
better (I'd) better get on my horse.
between between a rock and a hard place
between between jobs
between between the devil and the deep blue sea

bound bound to do something
bowel Don't get your bowels in an uproar!
bowl bowl someone over
boy fair-haired boy
brass get down to brass tacks
bread one's bread and butter
break break a code
break break a habit
break break a law
break break a record
break break camp
break break new ground
break break one's back (to do something)
break break one's habit
break break one's neck (to do something)
break break one's word
break break someone's fall
break break the bank
break break the habit
break break the law
break break the news (to someone)
break break up (with someone)
break make a break for something
break You're breaking my heart.
breath catch one's breath
breath Don't hold your breath.
breath Don't waste your breath.
breath get (enough) time to catch one's breath
breath I don't have time to catch my breath.
breath time to catch one's breath
breathe breathe one's last
breathe Don't breathe a word of this to anyone.
breathe hardly have time to breathe
breathe I don't have time to breathe.
brew brew a plot

brick hit (someone) like a ton of bricks
bridge water under the bridge
brim brimming with something
bring bring someone or something up
bring bring someone to justice
bring bring the house down
bring What brings you here?
Broadway on Broadway
brow sweat of one's brow
brush have a brush with something
built Rome wasn't built in a day.
bulk in bulk
bull bull in a china shop
bull hit the bull's-eye
bump goose bumps
burn burn someone up
burn get one's fingers burned
burn have money to burn
burst burst into flame(s)
burst burst with joy
bury dead and buried
business business end of something
business Business is business.
business get down to business
business Get your nose out of my business.
business I'm just minding my own business.
business It's business as usual.
business Keep your nose out of my business.
business Mind your own business.
business monkey business
business open for business
business place of business
bustle hustle and bustle
busy I've been keeping myself busy.
but all over but the shouting

cheer Three cheers!
cheese Say cheese!
chest get something off one's chest
chicken no spring chicken
child child's play
child expecting (a child)
chin take it on the chin
china bull in a china shop
chisel chisel someone out of something
circumstance under normal circumstances
city Can't fight city hall.
city (You) can't fight city hall.
claim claim a life
class cut class
clay have feet of clay
clean have clean hands
clear clear of something
clear clear the table
clear I read you loud and clear.
clock against the clock
close keep a close rein on someone or something
close play one's cards close to one's vest
closet come out of the closet
cloud under a cloud (of suspicion)
clutch in(to) someone's clutches
code break a code
cold catch cold
cold get cold feet
cold take cold
color horse of a different color
color horse of another color
coma lapse into a coma
comb go over something with a fine-tooth comb
comb search something with a fine-tooth comb
come as _____ as they come
come come across someone or something

come Come and get it!
come come apart at the seams
come come away empty-handed
come come down with something
come come into one's or its own
come Come off it!
come come out in the wash
come come out of the closet
come come to a dead end
come come to a head
come come to a stop
come come to the point
come come what may
come dream come true
come easy come, easy go
come Expect me when you see me (coming).
come First come, first served.
come if worst comes to worst
come some creature's time has come
come someone's time has come
come They must have seen you coming.
come You've got another think coming.
comedy Cut the comedy!
command have a good command of something
command have a poor command of something
company keep company
compliment fish for a compliment
compliment pay someone a compliment
compromise reach a compromise
concern (as) far as I'm concerned
concern far as I'm concerned
conclusion foregone conclusion
consider all things considered

consignment on consignment

conspicuous be conspicuous by one's absence

constant in a (constant) state of flux

construction under construction

contact have contact with someone

contempt in contempt (of court)

contention bone of contention

contest not going to win any beauty contests

context in the context of something

contrary contrary to something

control control the purse strings

control out of control

control under control

cook cook something to perfection

cook What's cooking?

cool Been keeping cool.

cool I'm cool.

cool (I've) been keeping cool.

cool Keeping cool.

could (Could I) give you a lift?

could Could I have a lift?

could Could I join you?

could Could you keep a secret?

could You could have fooled me.

could You could have knocked me over with a feather.

count count on someone or something

counter under the counter

couple couple of _____

courage muster (up) one's courage

course course of action

course take a course (in something)

court ball is in your court

court in contempt (of court)

court settle (something) (out of court)

cover blow someone's cover

cover cover a lot of ground

cover cover something up

crack crack a joke

crack get cracking (on something)

crazy crazy about someone or something

crazy drive someone crazy

crazy go crazy

credit Cash or credit (card)?

credit credit to someone or something

credit extend credit (to someone)

credit on credit

cross cross swords (with someone)

crux crux of the matter

cry cry bloody murder

cup not one's cup of tea

curiosity pique someone's curiosity

curl curl up and die

curry curry favor with someone

custody in custody

cut cut class

cut Cut it out!

cut cut school

cut cut someone off (short)

cut Cut the comedy!

cut Cut the funny stuff!

cut cut the ground out from under someone

damage What's the damage?

dance go into one's song and dance about something

danger fraught with danger

dare Don't you dare!

dare How dare you!

dark shot in the dark

dart dart in and out

date date back (to some time)

Davy go to Davy Jones's locker
dawn dawn on someone
dawn from dawn to dusk
day all in a day's work
day by day
day days running
day (Go ahead,) make my day!
day has seen better days
day I haven't got all day.
day in all my born days
day in this day and age
day It's just not my day!
day Make my day!
day one of these (fine) days
day order of the day
day Rome wasn't built in a day.
day That'll be the day!
dead beating a dead horse
dead come to a dead end
dead dead and buried
dead have someone dead to rights
dead in a dead heat
deal Big deal!
deal great deal
death at death's door
death be death on something
death death of someone
death death on someone or something
death meet one's death
death You'll be the death of me (yet).
debt in debt
debt pay one's debt to society
deem deem it (to be) necessary
deem deem that it is necessary
deep between the devil and the deep blue sea
defensive on the defensive
delight ravished with delight
den den of iniquity
denial in denial
depart depart (this life)
depth beyond one's depth

descend be descended from someone or some creature
desert desert a sinking ship
desert get one's just deserts
detail go into detail
detail in detail
devil between the devil and the deep blue sea
diaper soil one's diaper(s)
dibs have dibs on something
dice No dice!
die curl up and die
die die by one's own hand
die die of boredom
die die on the vine
different horse of a different color
dig Dig in!
dig dig up some dirt on someone
dirt dig up some dirt on someone
dirty air someone's dirty linen in public
disguise in disguise
dish do the dishes
dispose ill-disposed to doing something
distance go the distance
divert divert something into something
dog go to the dogs
dog raining cats and dogs
dollar almighty dollar
dollar feel like a million (dollars)
door answer the door
door at death's door
door beat a path to someone's door
door next-door neighbor
dose get a dose of one's own medicine
doubt benefit of the doubt
doubt beyond the shadow of a doubt

end hold up one's end (of the bargain)

end It's not the end of the world.

end make (both) ends meet

end meet one's end

end put an end to something

English plain English

enough Enough of that!

enough Enough said.

enough get (enough) time to catch one's breath

enough get up enough nerve (to do something)

entirety in its entirety

entirety in their entirety

errand run an errand

escape avenue of escape

even get even (with someone)

evening evening of life

event in the event of something

every every other person or thing

everything everything but the kitchen sink

everything everything from A to Z

everything everything from soup to nuts

everything everything humanly possible

evil lesser of two evils

excess do something to excess

excitement ripple of excitement

excuse excuse someone from something

existence in existence

expect expecting (a child)

expect Expect me when you see me (coming).

expect when least expected

expedition go on a fishing expedition

extend extend credit (to someone)

eye apple of someone's eye

eye catch someone's eye

eye eye of the storm

eye feast one's eyes (on someone or something)

eye get stars in one's eyes

eye have a good eye for something

eye have an eye for something

eye have an eye out (for someone or something)

eye have stars in one's eyes

eye hit someone (right) between the eyes

eye hit the bull's-eye

eye keep an eye out (for someone or something)

eye keep one's eye on someone or something

eyeball eyeball-to-eyeball

eyeful get an eyeful (of someone or something)

face face the music

face have egg on one's face

face take something at face value

face Wipe that smile off your face!

fact as a matter of fact

fact grounded in fact

fact in fact

fact known fact

fair fair-haired boy

fall break someone's fall

fall fall apart

fall fall asleep

fall fall between two stools

fall fall ill

fall fall in love

fall fall to someone

fallow lie fallow

false lull someone into a false sense of security

familiar familiar with someone or something

familiar have a familiar ring

finish from start to finish
fire catch fire
fire fire a gun
fire Fire away!
fire have too many irons in the fire
fire on fire
fire set fire to something
fire Where's the fire?
first First come, first served.
first first of all
first Not if I see you first.
fish fine kettle of fish
fish fish for a compliment
fish go on a fishing expedition
fish have bigger fish to fry
fish have other fish to fry
fit fit in with someone or something
fit fit like a glove
five Give me five!
five Slip me five!
fix in a fix
fix well-fixed
fixings with all the fixings
flame burst into flame(s)
flash in a flash
flatter flatter one's figure
flatter You flatter yourself.
flattery Flattery will get you nowhere.
flies There are no flies on someone.
flies time flies
flight in flight
flirt flirt with the idea of doing something
floor This is my floor.
flux in a (constant) state of flux
flux in flux
fly get off to a flying start
fly Go fly a kite!
fly I've got to fly.
fly There are no flies on someone.
fly time flies

foist foist something (off) on someone
follow Do you follow?
follow follow one's heart
follow follow one's nose
follow follow someone's lead
follow follow up (on something)
food food for thought
fool fool's paradise
fool You could have fooled me.
foot balls of one's feet
foot bound hand and foot
foot find one's feet
foot foot the bill
foot get cold feet
foot get one's feet on the ground
foot get to one's feet
foot have feet of clay
foot have one's feet on the ground
foot have the shoe on the other foot
foot on foot
foothold get a foothold (somewhere)
force join forces
forefront at the forefront (of something)
forefront in the forefront (of something)
foregone foregone conclusion
forget Forget it!
form form an opinion
fort hold the fort
forth and so forth
foul use foul language
fraught fraught with danger
fray join the fray
fray jump into the fray
free for free
free free and easy
free free gift
free free translation

get get an eyeful (of someone or something)
get get a rise out of someone
get get a word in edgeways
get get a word in edgewise
get get cold feet
get get cracking (on something)
get get down to brass tacks
get get down to business
get get down to work
get get (enough) time to catch one's breath
get get even (with someone)
get get fresh (with someone)
get get married
get get off on a sidetrack
get get off the hook
get get off to a flying start
get get one's feet on the ground
get get one's fingers burned
get get one's just deserts
get get one's second wind
get get on someone's nerves
get get out of the wrong side of the bed
get get rid of someone or something
get get someone's ear
get get something across (to someone)
get get something into someone's thick head
get get something off one's chest
get get something straight
get get something through someone's thick skull
get get something under way
get get stars in one's eyes
get get the drift of something
get get the feel of something
get get the final word
get get the last laugh
get get the last word
get get the runaround
get get the shock of one's life

get get the upper hand (on someone)
get getting on (in years)
get get to one's feet
get get to someone
get get to the point
get get up enough nerve (to do something)
get get up on the wrong side of the bed
get get wind of something
get Get your nose out of my business.
get (I'd) better get on my horse.
get I (just) don't get it.
get I've got to go home and get my beauty sleep.
get You can't get there from here.
gift free gift
give (Could I) give you a lift?
give Don't give it another thought.
give Don't give it a (second) thought.
give Don't give me that!
give Don't give up!
give Don't give up the ship!
give Don't give up too eas(il)y!
give Don't give up without a fight!
give give-and-take
give give birth to someone or some creature
give give birth to something
give Give me a chance!
give Give me five!
give Give me (some) skin!
give given
give given to doing something
give give one a new lease on life
give give (one's) notice
give give someone a blank check

good have a good command of something

good have a good eye for something

good have a good head on one's shoulders

good if you know what's good for you

good I've been up to no good.

good on good terms (with someone)

good put something to (good) use

good So far, so good.

goose goose bumps

goose goose pimples

gorge feel one's gorge rise

gorge make someone's gorge rise

gospel gospel truth

got have got a lot of nerve

got have got some nerve

got I haven't got all day.

got ill-gotten gains

got (It's) got me beat.

got I've got it!

got I've got to fly.

got I've got to go home and get my beauty sleep.

got I've got to run.

got I've got to split.

got I've got to take off.

got I've only got one pair of hands.

got You got me beat.

got You've got another think coming.

got You('ve) got me there.

gotten ill-gotten gains

grab grab a bite (to eat)

grace graced with something

grace grace someone or something with one's presence

grain against the grain

grain grain of truth

grate grate on someone('s nerves)

grave carry a secret to one's grave

grave carry a secret to the grave

great great deal

grind grind to a halt

grindstone keep one's nose to the grindstone

grip grip someone's attention

grit grit one's teeth

groan groan under the weight of something

ground break new ground

ground cover a lot of ground

ground cut the ground out from under someone

ground get one's feet on the ground

ground grounded in fact

ground grounds for something

ground have one's feet on the ground

ground keep one's ear to the ground

grow grow to do something

grudge hold a grudge (against someone)

grunt grunt work

guess hazard a guess

guest Be my guest.

guest guest of honor

guilty feel guilty (about something)

guilty find someone guilty

gulp gulp for air

gun beat the gun

gun fire a gun

gun pull a gun (on someone)

gut gut feeling

gut gut reaction

gut gut response

gut hate someone's guts

gyp gyp someone out of something

have have a bee in one's bonnet

have have a bone to pick (with someone)

have have a brush with something

have have a familiar ring

have have a frog in one's throat

have have a go at something

have have a good command of something

have have a good eye for something

have have a good head on one's shoulders

have have a hand in something

have have a handle on something

have have a head for something

have have a heart

have have a heart of gold

have have a hold on someone

have have a look at someone or something

have have a look for someone or something

have have an ear for something

have have an eye for something

have have an eye out (for someone or something)

have have an in (with someone)

have have an itch for something

have have an itch to do something

have have a nose for something

have have a one-track mind

have have a passion for someone or something

have have a peep

have have a penchant for something

have have a poor command of something

have have arrived

have have a run-in with someone

have have a stab at something

have have a sweet tooth

have have a taste for something

have Have at it.

have have a vested interest in something

have have a weight problem

have have a word with someone

have have bats in one's belfry

have have bigger fish to fry

have have clean hands

have have contact with someone

have have dibs on something

have have egg on one's face

have have feet of clay

have have got a lot of nerve

have have got some nerve

have have money to burn

have have nothing to do with someone or something

have have one's back to the wall

have have one's feet on the ground

have have one's finger in the pie

have have one's finger in the till

have have one's hand in the till

have have one's heart in one's mouth

have have one's heart set on something

have have one's nose in a book

have have one's sights trained on something

have have other fish to fry

have have second thoughts about someone or something

have have [some] bearing on something

have have someone dead to rights

heart one's heart goes out to someone

heart one's heart is in one's mouth

heart with all one's heart and soul

heart You're breaking my heart.

heartbeat do something in a heartbeat

heartbeat heartbeat away from something

hearty hale and hearty

heat in a dead heat

heaven in heaven

heaven in seventh heaven

heavy Time hangs heavy on someone's hands.

heeled well-heeled

height at the height of something

hell give someone hell

helm at the helm (of something)

help cannot help doing something

help help oneself (to something)

help lend (someone) a helping hand

help Not if I can help it.

help seek professional help

here Fancy meeting you here!

here Here we go again.

here Here you are.

here What brings you here?

here Where do we go from here?

here You can't get there from here.

hide go into hiding

high hold someone or something in high regard

high running high

highly speak highly of someone or something

highly think highly of someone or something

hike take a hike

hinge hinge on something

hire new hire

hire not for hire

history go down in history

history rest is history

hit hit a plateau

hit hit home

hit hit it off (with someone)

hit hit someone hard

hit hit (someone) like a ton of bricks

hit hit someone (right) between the eyes

hit hit the bull's-eye

hit hit the nail (right) on the head

hit hit the sack

hitch hitch a ride

hive hive of activity

hock go into hock

hock in hock

hold Don't hold your breath.

hold have a hold on someone

hold hold a grudge (against someone)

hold hold one's end (of the bargain) up

hold hold one's peace

hold hold one's tongue

hold hold someone hostage

hold hold someone or something in high regard

hold hold someone's attention

hold hold the fort

hold hold up one's end (of the bargain)

hold Hold your horses!

hold on hold

hold put a hold on something

hole poke a hole in something

hole poke a hole through something

hole punch a hole in something

incline inclined to do something

incumbent incumbent (up)on someone to do something

influence under the influence

influence under the influence of someone or something

iniquity den of iniquity

initiative take the initiative

injury add insult to injury

ink in ink

innocent find someone innocent

innocent play innocent

insane drive someone insane

instance for instance

insult add insult to injury

insult hurl an insult (at someone)

intent intent on doing something

interest have a vested interest in something

interest of interest (to someone)

interest pique someone's interest

interim in the interim (between things)

interval at regular intervals

into burst into flame(s)

into come into one's or its own

into divert something into something

into get something into someone's thick head

into go into detail

into go into hiding

into go into hock

into go into one's song and dance about something

into in(to) a jam

into into being

into in(to) someone's clutches

into jump into the fray

into lapse into a coma

into lull someone into a false sense of security

into put some teeth into something

into send someone into some state

into talk someone into doing something

into throw something into the bargain

into trick someone into doing something

invasion invasion of one's privacy

inventory take inventory

invest invest someone's time in something

invest invest someone with something

invest invest something in someone or something

invite invite someone to resign

iron have too many irons in the fire

issue issue a call for something

itch have an itch for something

itch have an itch to do something

itself end in itself

itself shadow of itself

jam in(to) a jam

jeopardy in jeopardy

jiffy in a jiffy

jig jig is up

job between jobs

jog jog someone's memory

join Could I join you?

join (Do you) mind if I join you?

join If you can't lick 'em, join 'em.

join join forces

join join hands

join join the fray

join Mind if I join you?

joke (all) joking aside

know I didn't know you cared.
know I don't know about that!
know if you know what's good for you
know I know just how you feel!
know I know the feeling.
know know something in one's bones
know know the score
know know what's what
know let someone know (about something)
know not know when one is well off
know One never knows.
know (Well,) what do you know!
know What do you know?
know What do you know for sure?
know You know what?
knowledge to the best of my knowledge
known known fact
known known quantity
labor fruit(s) of one's labor(s)
labor in labor
ladder at the bottom of the ladder
lake Go jump in the lake!
land on land
language use foul language
lapse lapse into a coma
lark for a lark
lark on a lark
last at last
last at the last minute
last breathe one's last
last get the last laugh
last get the last word
last last (one)
last pay one's last respects
last see the last of someone or something
last That's the last straw!
last very last

later Catch me later.
laugh Don't make me laugh!
laugh get the last laugh
laundry in the laundry
lavatory go to the lavatory
law break a law
law break the law
lay lay down one's life for something
lay lay someone off
lay lay someone to rest
lay lay something to waste
lay lay waste to something
lead blind leading the blind
lead follow someone's lead
lead leading question
league in league (with someone)
lean lean toward doing something
lease give one a new lease on life
least when least expected
leave leave a sinking ship
leave leave one's mark on someone
left better left unsaid
leg with one's tail between one's legs
lend lend someone a hand
lend lend (someone) a helping hand
lesser lesser (of the two)
lesser lesser of two evils
let I'll let you go.
let let go of someone or something
let let out a sound
let Let's do lunch (sometime).
let let someone go
let let someone know (about something)
let let something pass
let let something slide (by)
let let something slip (by)
let Let's shake on it.

look I'm just looking.
look I'm only looking.
look look down on someone or something
look take a look at someone or something
look take a look for someone or something
lookout on the lookout for someone or something
lose lose one's mind
lose lose one's temper (at someone or something)
lose lose one's train of thought
lose lose track (of someone or something)
lot cover a lot of ground
lot draw lots
lot get a lot of mileage out of something
lot have got a lot of nerve
lot lot of
lot lots of
loud I read you loud and clear.
love fall in love
lovely Lovely weather for ducks.
low run low (on something)
lower lower oneself to some level
luck press one's luck
lull lull before the storm
lull lull someone into a false sense of security
lull lull someone to sleep
lunch Let's do lunch (sometime).
lunch We('ll) have to do lunch sometime.
lung at the top of one's lungs
mad in a mad rush
mad like mad
mad mad about someone or something
mad mad for someone or something
mad steaming (mad)

mainstream in the mainstream (of something)
make Don't make me laugh!
make (Go ahead,) make my day!
make have the makings of something
make make a break for something
make make a friend
make make a living by doing something
make make a living from something
make make allowances for someone
make make allowances for something
make make amends (for something)
make make a pass at someone
make make (both) ends meet
make make friends
make make fun of someone or something
make make it
make make it worth someone's while
make Make my day!
make make overtures
make make someone's gorge rise
make make someone's head spin
make make something up
make make up for something
make make up (with someone)
make make use of someone or something
make what makes someone tick
make what makes something tick
makings have the makings of something
man marked man

monkey monkey around
monkey monkey (around) with something
monkey monkey business
month I haven't seen you in a month of Sundays.
month months running
mood in the mood for something
mood in the mood to do something
moon ask for the moon
more more and more
most at (the) most
motion table a motion
mouth have one's heart in one's mouth
mouth one's heart is in one's mouth
mouth Watch your mouth!
mouth You took the words right out of my mouth.
mouthful You (really) said a mouthful.
move It's your move.
much Not (too) much.
murder cry bloody murder
murder murder on something
murder scream bloody murder
music face the music
music set something to music
music Stop the music!
must They must have seen you coming.
muster muster (up) one's courage
myself I've been keeping myself busy.
nail hit the nail (right) on the head
name call someone names
name drop names
name I didn't catch the name.
name I didn't catch your name.
name What was the name again?

nap take a nap
nature call of nature
necessary deem it (to be) necessary
necessary deem that it is necessary
neck break one's neck (to do something)
neck up to one's neck (in something)
neck yoke around someone's neck
need in need
need in need of something
needle needle in a haystack
neighbor next-door neighbor
neighborhood in the neighborhood of something
neighborhood (somewhere) in the neighborhood of something
neither neither does someone
nerve get on someone's nerves
nerve get up enough nerve (to do something)
nerve grate on someone('s nerves)
nerve have got a lot of nerve
nerve have got some nerve
neutral in neutral
never Never fear!
never One never knows.
never Will wonders never cease?
new break new ground
new give one a new lease on life
new new blood
new new hire
new (So) what else is new?
new What else is new?
news break the news (to someone)
next next-door neighbor
next next of kin
next next to nothing

oath take an oath
oath under oath
occasion on occasion
ocean ocean of someone or something
ocean oceans of someone or something
odd odd something
offense take offense at someone or something
old be old hat
old old hand at doing something
once I can only do so many things at once.
once if I've told you once, I've told you a thousand times
one back to square one
one go in one ear and out the other
one have a one-track mind
one in one fell swoop
one I owe you one.
one I've heard that one before.
one I've only got one pair of hands.
one last (one)
one one final thing
one one final word
one one of these (fine) days
one one thing or person after another
oneself avail oneself of something
oneself beside oneself
oneself fend for oneself
oneself gear (oneself) up for something
oneself help oneself (to something)
oneself lower oneself to some level
oneself pride oneself on something
oneself reconcile oneself to something

oneself shadow of oneself
oneself suit oneself
only I can only do so many things at once.
only I'm only looking.
only I've only got one pair of hands.
open in the open
open open book
open open for business
open opening gambit
open open to something
opinion form an opinion
opinion hazard an opinion
opinion I'll thank you to keep your opinions to yourself.
opinion in my opinion
order call a meeting to order
order order of the day
order place an order
other Catch me some other time.
other drop the other shoe
other every other person or thing
other from the other side of the tracks
other go in one ear and out the other
other have other fish to fry
other have the shoe on the other foot
other other place
other turn the other cheek
outright killed outright
outset at the outset
outset from the outset
outside at the outside
over (all) over again
over all over but the shouting
over bowl someone over
over go over someone's head
over go over something with a fine-tooth comb
over have someone over

peep take a peep
peeve pet peeve
peg have someone pegged as something
peg peg someone as something
penchant have a penchant for something
pencil in pencil
people number of things or people
per per head
perfection cook something to perfection
permit weather permitting
perpetuity in perpetuity
persist persist in doing something
persist persist with something
person every other person or thing
person in person
person one thing or person after another
person on one's person
person shuttle someone or something from person to person
personally take something personally
perspective perspective on something
persuasion be of the persuasion that . . .
pet pet hate
pet pet peeve
pet teacher's pet
pick have a bone to pick (with someone)
pick pick a lock
pick pick of something
picture Do I have to paint (you) a picture?
picture picture of something
pie have one's finger in the pie
piece give someone a piece of one's mind

piece piece of cake
pierce piercing scream
pillar pillar of strength
pillar pillar of support
pimple goose pimples
pinch in a pinch
piping piping hot
pique pique someone's curiosity
pique pique someone's interest
pitch pitch black
pitch pitch camp
pitch pitch one's tent
pity take pity on someone
place between a rock and a hard place
place in place of someone or something
place not one's place
place on one's way (to something or some place)
place on the way (to something or some place)
place other place
place place an order
place place of business
place see someone to some place
place shuttle someone or something from place to place
place stranger to something or some place
place sweep out of some place
place take place
place talk of some place
plain plain English
plateau hit a plateau
play at play
play child's play
play play a joke on someone
play play a trick on someone
play play ignorant
play play innocent
play play one's cards close to one's vest

put put one's mind to something
put put one's oar in
put put one's shoulder to the wheel
put put someone off
put put someone on
put put someone or something to the test
put put someone to bed
put put some teeth into something
put put something off
put put something on
put put something to bed
put put something to (good) use
put put up with someone or something
putty putty in someone's hands
quake quake in one's boots
quantity known quantity
question field questions
question leading question
question pose a question
quiet Better keep quiet about it.
quit call it quits
quite quite a few
quote quote a price
rack racked with pain
rail rail at someone (about something)
rain pouring rain
rain raining cats and dogs
rampage go on a rampage
rampant run rampant
random at random
rant rant (at someone) about someone or something
rap rap with someone
rap take the rap (for something)
rate at any rate
rate going rate
rather would rather

ravish ravished with delight
reach reach a compromise
reach reach an agreement
reach reach an impasse
reaction gut reaction
read I read you loud and clear.
real real thing
reality in reality
really I'm (really) fed up (with someone or something).
really You (really) said a mouthful.
rear at the rear of something
rear in the rear
receipt in receipt of something
recent in recent memory
recognize recognize one for what one is
recognize recognize something for what it is
reconcile reconcile oneself to something
record break a record
red roll out the red carpet (for someone)
reduce reduced to something
regard hold someone or something in high regard
regard with regard to someone or something
regardless regardless of something
regular at regular intervals
rehearsal in rehearsal
rein keep a close rein on someone or something
rein keep a tight rein on someone or something
reliance reliance on someone or something
relieve relieve one of one's duties
religious religious about doing something
relish with relish

run run out of patience
run run out of something
run run rampant
run run short (of something)
run Run that by me again.
run weeks running
run years running
runaround get the runaround
runaround give someone the runaround
rush in a mad rush
rush rush on something
rut in a rut
rut (stuck) in a rut
sack hit the sack
safe be on the safe side
safekeeping for safekeeping
sage sage advice
said Enough said.
said You (really) said a mouthful.
sail set sail (for somewhere)
sake for someone's or something's sake
sake for the sake of someone or something
salad toss a salad
sale for sale
sale on sale
same same as someone or something
sand sands of time
say Anything you say.
say as the saying goes
say Enough said.
say I hear what you're saying.
say Say cheese!
say Smile when you say that.
say That's easy for you to say.
say What do you say?
say You can say that again!
say You don't say.
say You (really) said a mouthful.
scale scale something down
scale scale something up
schedule behind schedule

school cut school
school school of thought
score know the score
scout scout around for someone or something
scrape scrape something together
scrape scrape something up
scream piercing scream
scream scream bloody murder
scrutiny under scrutiny
sea at sea
sea at sea (about something)
sea at sea level
sea between the devil and the deep blue sea
seal My lips are sealed.
seam come apart at the seams
search Search me.
search search something with a fine-tooth comb
seat show one to one's seat
seat show someone to a seat
second Don't give it a (second) thought.
second get one's second wind
second have second thoughts about someone or something
secret carry a secret to one's grave
secret carry a secret to the grave
secret Could you keep a secret?
secret in secret
secret keep a secret
security lull someone into a false sense of security
security security against something
see Am I glad to see you!
see as I see it
see Expect me when you see me (coming).
see has seen better days
see I haven't seen you in a month of Sundays.

show show one to one's seat
show show someone to a seat
show show something off
shower take a shower
shuttle shuttle someone or something from person to person
shuttle shuttle someone or something from place to place
shy shy away from someone or something
sick sick (and tired) of someone or something
side be on the safe side
side from side to side
side from the other side of the tracks
side get out of the wrong side of the bed
side get up on the wrong side of the bed
sidetrack get off on a sidetrack
sight have one's sights trained on something
sight in sight
sight partially sighted
sight train one's sights on something
since since time immemorial
sink desert a sinking ship
sink everything but the kitchen sink
sink leave a sinking ship
sit sit around (somewhere)
sit sit idly by
sketch thumbnail sketch
skin Give me (some) skin!
skin no skin off someone's nose
skin Skin me!
skin Slip me some skin!
skip hop, skip, and a jump
skip skip rope
skull get something through someone's thick skull
slave be a slave to something

sleep I've got to go home and get my beauty sleep.
sleep lull someone to sleep
slide let something slide (by)
slip let something slip (by)
slip Slip me five!
slip Slip me some skin!
slow slow going
slower slower and slower
small be a big frog in a small pond
small be thankful for small blessings
smile Smile when you say that.
smile Wipe that smile off your face!
snuff not up to snuff
so and so forth
so and so on
so I can only do so many things at once.
so if so
so Not so fast!
so So far, so good.
so so long as
so (So) what else is new?
society pay one's debt to society
sock Stuff a sock in it!
soil soil one's diaper(s)
sold sold out
some Catch me some other time.
some dig up some dirt on someone
some Give me (some) skin!
some have got some nerve
some have [some] bearing on something
some in some respects
some put some teeth into something
some shed some light on something
some Slip me some skin!
somehow work out (somehow)

storage in storage
storm eye of the storm
storm lull before the storm
straight get something straight
straight go straight
straight vote a straight ticket
stranger stranger to something or some place
straw That's the last straw!
strength pillar of strength
stretch stretch the truth
strike go (out) on strike
strike have two strikes against one
strike it strikes me that . . .
strike strike a pose
strike strike home
strike strike someone as something
string control the purse strings
stuck (stuck) in a rut
stuff Cut the funny stuff!
stuff Stuff a sock in it!
stupor in a stupor
style out of style
subject subject to something
succumb succumb to something
such as such
suggestive suggestive of something
suit suit oneself
Sunday I haven't seen you in a month of Sundays.
sunset one's sunset years
supply in short supply
support pillar of support
suppose It's not supposed to.
suppose Someone's not supposed to.
suppose supposed to do something
sure What do you know for sure?
surgery in surgery

surprise take someone by surprise
susceptible susceptible to something
suspicion under a cloud (of suspicion)
sweat Don't sweat it!
sweat sweat of one's brow
sweep sweep out of some place
sweet have a sweet tooth
sweet You bet your (sweet) life!
swim be swimming in something
swoop in one fell swoop
sword cross swords (with someone)
system All systems are go.
table clear the table
table set the table
table table a motion
tack get down to brass tacks
tail with one's tail between one's legs
take as a duck takes to water
take give-and-take
take I've got to take off.
take take a bath
take take a chance
take take a course (in something)
take take advantage of someone
take take advantage of something
take take a fancy to someone or something
take take a hike
take take a look at someone or something
take take a look for someone or something
take take a nap
take take an oath
take take a peep
take take a potshot at someone or something

that Don't give me that!
that Enough of that!
that for all the good that will do you
that How about that!
that I don't know about that!
that Imagine that!
that it strikes me that . . .
that I've heard that one before.
that powers that be
that provided that . . .
that Run that by me again.
that see (to it) that something is done
that Smile when you say that.
that That'll be the day!
that That's easy for you to say.
that That's the last straw!
that That's the ticket!
that That takes the cake!
that turn out (that)
that What does that prove?
that Wipe that smile off your face!
that You can say that again!
their in their entirety
then now and then
theory in theory
there all there
there over there
there There are no flies on someone.
there There, now.
there There, there.
there There you are.
there There you go!
there (way) over there
there You can't get there from here.
there You('ve) got me there.
these one of these (fine) days
they as _____ as they come
thick get something into someone's thick head
thick get something through someone's thick skull

thing all things considered
thing every other person or thing
thing I can only do so many things at once.
thing in the interim (between things)
thing number of things or people
thing one final thing
thing one thing or person after another
thing real thing
thing seeing things
thing very thing
think think highly of someone or something
think Think nothing of it.
think You've got another think coming.
thirst thirst for something
thirsty thirsty for something
this depart (this life)
this Don't breathe a word of this to anyone.
this in this day and age
this This is my floor.
this This one's on me.
thought Don't give it another thought.
thought Don't give it a (second) thought.
thought food for thought
thought have second thoughts about someone or something
thought lose one's train of thought
thought school of thought
thousand if I've told you once, I've told you a thousand times
thread thread one's way through something
thread thread through something
three Three cheers!

tooth go over something with a fine-tooth comb
tooth grit one's teeth
tooth have a sweet tooth
tooth put some teeth into something
tooth search something with a fine-tooth comb
top at the top of one's lungs
top at the top of one's voice
top Can you top that?
top from the top
torn torn between something and something else
toss toss a salad
touch keep in touch (with someone or something)
touch remain in touch (with someone or something)
touch stay in touch (with someone or something)
tow in tow
toward lean toward doing something
town go to town
track from the other side of the tracks
track have a one-track mind
track lose track (of someone or something)
track on the right track
trade tricks of the trade
train have one's sights trained on something
train lose one's train of thought
train train one's sights on something
transit in transit
translation free translation
trap set a trap
travesty travesty of justice
tree barking up the wrong tree
trick one's bag of tricks
trick play a trick on someone
trick tricks of the trade

trick trick someone into doing something
triplicate in triplicate
trouble in trouble
trouble I've been keeping out of trouble.
true dream come true
trust in the trust of someone
trust misplace one's trust (in someone)
trust Trust me!
truth gospel truth
truth grain of truth
truth stretch the truth
try try one's wings (out)
tune in tune
tune out of tune
turn in turn
turn take turns (at something)
turn take turns (doing something)
turn take turns (with something)
turn turn of the century
turn turn out (that)
turn turn the other cheek
two fall between two stools
two have two strikes against one
two lesser (of the two)
two lesser of two evils
type set type
umbrage take umbrage at something
unaccustomed unaccustomed to someone or something
under cut the ground out from under someone
under get something under way
under groan under the weight of something
under have something under way
under under a cloud (of suspicion)

waste Don't waste your time.
waste lay something to waste
waste lay waste to something
watch Watch it!
watch watch one's step
watch watch over someone or something
watch watch someone or something like a hawk
watch Watch your mouth!
watch Watch your tongue!
watch will bear watching
water as a duck takes to water
water water under the bridge
way by the way
way get something under way
way have something under way
way on one's way (to something or some place)
way on the way (to something or some place)
way rub someone the wrong way
way thread one's way through something
way (way) over there
we as we speak
we Don't call us, we'll call you.
we Here we go again.
we Off we go.
we We aim to please.
we We just can't take you anywhere anymore.
we We('ll) have to do lunch sometime.
we Where do we go from here?
wealth wealth of something
wear I don't want to wear out my welcome.
wear wear and tear
weather Lovely weather for ducks.
weather under the weather
weather weather permitting
wedded wed(ded) to someone
wedded wedded to something

wedlock born out of wedlock
week weeks running
weight groan under the weight of something
weight have a weight problem
weight worth one's or its weight in gold
welcome I don't want to wear out my welcome.
welcome welcome to do something
welcome You are welcome.
well as well
well as well as
well not know when one is well off
well well-fixed
well well-heeled
well well-off
well (Well,) what do you know!
were if I were you
what come what may
what if you know what's good for you
what I hear what you're saying.
what know what's what
what recognize one for what one is
what recognize something for what it is
what (So) what else is new?
what (Well,) what do you know!
what What are you drinking?
what What brings you here?
what What does that prove?
what What do you know?
what What do you know for sure?
what What do you say?
what What else is new?
what What for?
what What gives?
what what if
what what makes someone tick

world It's not the end of the world.

worst if worst comes to worst

worth make it worth someone's while

worth worth one's or its weight in gold

would I wouldn't dream of it!

would would like (to have) someone or something

would would rather

would Yesterday wouldn't be too soon.

wreak wreak vengeance (up)on someone or something

wrong barking up the wrong tree

wrong Don't get me wrong.

wrong get out of the wrong side of the bed

wrong get up on the wrong side of the bed

wrong rub someone the wrong way

yarn spin a yarn

year advanced in years

year getting on (in years)

year one's sunset years

year year after year

year years running

yesterday Yesterday wouldn't be too soon.

yet You ain't seen nothing yet!

yet You'll be the death of me (yet).

yoke yoke around someone's neck

young not as young as one used to be

yourself I hope you are proud of yourself!

yourself I'll thank you to keep your opinions to yourself.

yourself Take care (of yourself).

yourself Where (have) you been keeping yourself?

yourself You flatter yourself.

Z everything from A to Z

zenith at the zenith of something